Other Books by Eugene C. Rollins

Grace Is Not a Blue-Eyed Blonde
2008

The Masks We Wear
2010

The Power of the Spoken Word
2011

Taming My Tongue
2011

Why I Take the Bible Seriously But Not Literally
2016

When Life Tumbles In, What Then?

WOUNDED WOUNDER
or
WOUNDED HEALER

DR. EUGENE C. ROLLINS

authorHOUSE®

AuthorHouse™
1663 Liberty Drive
Bloomington, IN 47403
www.authorhouse.com
Phone: 833-262-8899

Published by AuthorHouse 09/11/2020

ISBN: 978-1-7283-6907-5 (sc)
ISBN: 978-1-7283-7015-6 (e)

Print information available on the last page.

DEDICATION

I dedicate this book to the hundreds of wounded people I have worked with over the last fifty-three years. Some were healed and some were not. Some became healers and some remained wounders. But all of them have contributed to my continued healing. I thank the Great Healer for their tracks left upon my life and ministry.
Gene Rollins

CONTENTS

Origin of the Book

This book was first prepared as sermons and was delivered at lakeside worship on Wateree Lake in Kershaw County, South Carolina. Liberty Hill Presbyterian Church (PCUSA) began this outreach in July of 1977. I was pastor of the church from May 1984 until January 1, 2012.

Preaching is a verbal art not a written art. In the history of preaching, sermons were prepared orally to be delivered orally. The most frequent criticism I hear about preachers is that "he reads his sermons." These sermons were delivered orally, taped and then transcribed into written form. The sermon outline is the only written thing I carry to the pulpit other than my Bible. Transcribing the oral word into the written word is difficult. Many thanks to Mrs. Sylvia Hudson who did the transcribing. It is fully to her credit that these spoken sermons now appear in print.

The outline, or what I call the "Sermon Syllabus," is fully explained in my book, "Grace Is Not a Blue-Eyed Blond," chapter 2, pages 3-8. I put a copy of the Sermon Syllabus in the church bulletin each worship so the people can track where I am going and also help them remember the message. I include it in the printed sermons with the same hope that it will help you in following my thoughts.

All major religions have a path from woundedness to healing. My path is the Jesus path. Jesus said to Peter: "Peter, you must be ground like wheat, and once you have recovered, then you can turn and help the brothers." (Luke 22:31-32)
Gene Rollins

My Theology of Life

There are three types of people in the world; sheep, wolves and shepherds. We are all born sheep. As sheep we are all wounded in some form and to some degree. If our wounds are left unattended we become victims of life. If our wounds are agitated and left unhealed and unredeemed we become wolves. If our wounds are acknowledged, healed and redeemed we become shepherds.

Wounded Healers or Wounded Wounders? It is our choice!

WHAT HAPPENS TO US IS NOT THAT IMPORTANT.

**IT IS WHAT HAPPENS TO WHAT HAPPENS
TO US THAT IS IMPORTANT.**

Carl Jung's archetype of the "wounded healer" originated with the Greek myth of Chiron who was physically wounded, and by way of overcoming the pain of his own wounds Chiron became the compassionate teacher of healing. But the greatest "wounded healer" the world has ever known is Jesus the Christ who heals humanity's wounds of sin through his death on the cross. "He was wounded for our transgressions....and with his stripes we are healed." (Isaiah 53:5)

CHAPTER 1

A BRIEF HISTORY OF WOUNDEDNESS

Text: 1 Peter 4:12-19 & 5:6-11 (All Scripture references are from
the New International Version)

CIT: *(Central Idea of the text)*
Suffering may drive a person to bitterness, to resentment, to
despair or it may make the person strong, firm and steadfast.

Thesis: Woundedness and sufferings are givens in life; what we do
with them is the unknown.

Purpose
- Major Objective: Supportive
- Specific Objective: Through the power of the Holy
Spirit, I hope to lead each of us in growing through our
woundedness and suffering.

Introduction

Outline:
    I.   The Buddhist Tradition
        A. Woundedness
        B. Healing
    II.   The Jewish Tradition
        A. Woundedness
        B. Healing

"We need not be overcome
by our wounds.
We need not perpetuate our own
wounds onto others through brutality –
verbal abuse or physical abuse.
There is healing."

Dr. Eugene C. Rollins

The Word of the Lord

1 Peter 4:12-19

12 Dear friends, do not be surprised at the painful trial you're suffering as though something strange were happening to you. 13 But rejoice that you participate in the sufferings of Christ, so that you may be overjoyed when his glory is revealed. 14 If you are insulted because of the name of Christ, you are blessed, for the spirit of glory and of God rests on you. 15 If you suffer, it should not be as a murderer or a thief or any other kind of criminal, or even as a meddler. 16 However, if you suffer as a Christian, do not be ashamed, but praise God that you bear that name. 17 For it is time for judgment to begin with the family of God; and if it begins with us, what will the outcome be for those who do not obey the gospel of God? 18 And, "if it is hard for the righteous to be saved, what will become of the ungodly and the sinner?"

19 So then, those who suffer according to God's will should commit themselves to their faithful Creator and continue to do good.

I Peter 5:6-11

6 Humble yourselves, therefore, under God's Mighty hand, that he might lift you up in due time. 7 Cast all your anxiety on him because he cares for you. 8 Be self-controlled and alert. Your enemy the devil prowls around like a roaring lion looking for someone to devour. 9 Resist him, standing firm in the faith, because you know that your brothers throughout the world are undergoing the same kind of sufferings. 10 And the God of all grace, who called you to his eternal glory in Christ, after you have suffered a little while, will himself restore you and make you strong, firm and steadfast. 11 To him be the power forever and ever. Amen.

Introduction

Almost all of my adult life I have worked with the wounded: 49 years in the ministry through the church, 12 years with the South Carolina Department of Mental Health, 9 years with a general hospital, 15 years with the South Carolina Department of Corrections, and 35 years in a private psychotherapy practice. And the question that is constantly with me and has been with me over these many years is, "How and why do some who are wounded find healing in their wounds and become healers out of their wounds to other persons?" And then, "Why and how is it that others in and out of their wounds do not experience healing and they go on to become wounderers of other people out of their own wounds?" These are constant questions.

The research shows that those who abused children, higher than 79% were abused as children.[1] The research shows that the priests who sexually abused their altar boys were sexually abused as altar boys themselves. So, how is it that we come to embrace our wounds in such a way that we find enough healing that we use our wounded experiences to become Healers to other people and not perpetuate our wounds on to other people?

The concept of woundedness and healing has a long history. It was the psychiatrist Carl Jung who took the Greek myth of Chiron and made it popular. In that mythological story, Kronos, who was a god becomes a horse and rapes this mortal woman who bears a son, Chiron, who is half horse and half human - a Centaur. He is immediately abandoned by his mother at birth and lives a life of woundedness and at one point is shot in the knee by a poison arrow dipped in Hydro's blood. And out of those immense pains and sufferings, Chiron becomes a healer himself and a teacher of healers. He is filled with compassion and out of that compassion has the ability to reach out to others.[2]

The Shaman predates the physicians, the priests, and the medicine man. The Shaman embraces all three. The Shaman was the original spiritual guide, leader and the original medicine man, doctor, in the culture. The thread that goes all the way through Shamanism crosses cultures throughout the planet in time and space. The shaman is always deeply, deeply wounded - even to death and resurrection in some societies. And it is knowing the hurt, the pain, the suffering, knowing those wounds and owning those wounds and recognizing healing comes in the context of those wounds, therefore the Shaman becomes a healer.

---

[1] Gartner, Richard. B., Betrayed as Boys. New York, the Guilford Press, 1999, p. 80.

[2] Jung, C.G. The Practice of Psychotherapy. New York, Princeton University Press, 1954, p. 220.

In many cultures I have read the common title for the Shaman was Healer Madman, often considered to be "crazy." [3]

I. The Buddhist Tradition

The history of woundedness is almost as old as our society, the gathering of humankind itself. So, therefore, it is not surprising to me that the five major religions have within them characteristically that sense of woundedness and the sense of the potential of being healed. Take for example the Buddhist position. The original Buddha, Siddhartha, was a prince and had lived all of his life inside a palace and inside the walls. He lived all of his life in the context of luxury and all kinds of excesses. As a young man, Siddhartha left the confines of the palace to seek what was outside there in the world. Immediately he was exposed to suffering as he left the tranquility and serenity of the palace. He was thrown headlong into sickness. He was thrown headlong into the awareness of death and aging. And the first premise of Buddhist theology and understanding is, suffering exists. So it became Siddhartha's lifelong mission to come to understand suffering and not be consumed by suffering but allow that suffering to enlighten.[4]

II. The Jewish Tradition

The Jewish culture - our Christian Foundation - is literally filled with story after story of Israel and individuals within it. Israel undergoes immense suffering only to discover, out of suffering and enlightenment was healing. I could give you all kinds of examples and will give you quite a few this summer.

The Joseph story - rejected by his siblings, sold into slavery, placed into jail – he had nothing of his own. He was unjustly treated - wounded, but then out of his wounds became the Pharaoh's favorite son and becomes a healer to his own people.

---

[3] Campbell, Joseph. The Masks of God: Primitive Mythology. New York, The Viking Press, 1957, pp. 229-281.
[4] Hanh, Thick Nhat. The Heart of the Buddha's Teaching. Berkeley, California, Parallax Press, 1998.

Jeremiah, that major prophet who was called the weeping prophet, who preached so compassionately, says these words in the 10th chapter of Jeremiah. They are so profound: "Woe to me because of my injury. My wound is incurable. Yet, I said to myself this is my sickness and I must endure it." (Jeremiah 10:19) [5]

III. The Hindu Tradition

Over and over through the Jewish literature we see suffering and then healing, although not with all of them. We'll look at some of those cases later - Buddhists background, Jewish background. We often don't think about the Hindu tradition. But as Judaism gave rise to Christianity, Hinduism gave rise to Buddhism. Here is a classic statement in Hindu theology: "Your glory lies where you cease to exist. Your glory is found in the context of you *(and they're talking about big ego)* ceasing to exist." A powerful, powerful statement. It is woven all through the Hindu understanding of faith, God, and humankind.[6]

IV. The Muslim Tradition

When we think of the Muslim tradition we are so caught up in one word, and that is Jihad. We so misuse that word. Some of their fundamentalists misuse it and so have we. In the original word "Jihad" it means to struggle within oneself with that call to be submitted to the will of God and to our own ego, the self-centered "I" within all of us. The original meaning of the word "Jihad" was that struggle which takes place inside. It's become so common now that in their tradition they have two words. Jahar, the greater Jihad, which is that struggle within us and the Lesser Jihad which is that struggle with culture. I will give you a quote from their context out of the Quran. A powerful statement. "Die before death and resurrect now." Think of that. Die now to that big

---

[5] Limburg, James. Judaism: An Introduction for Christians. Minneapolis, Augsburg Publishing House, 1987.
[6] Pelikan, Jaroslav (ED). The World Treasury of Modern Religious Thought. Boston, Little Brown and Company, 1990, pp.490-497

selfish ego within you. Die now in the context of your bloodiness and woundedness and resurrect into something new, changed and different.[7]

V. The Christian Tradition

All of the religious traditions have within them this concept of being wounded and the potential out of that woundedness to find healing and then to go on to be a healer to others. But there's no more beautiful example, tragic though it is, than in our own story. Jesus, the God-man. God loving us so much that God became one of us, in the Christ and lived among us as a sinless teacher of morals, ethics, and psychology for living. And in the context of that kind of life, was mortally wounded on Calvary's tree. And the prophecy was fulfilled that our transgressions were placed upon him. Him who heals our sin. Him who heals our bruises. No greater model than Jesus the Christ, the wounded healer, who heals us in grace that we might embrace our healing, embrace our wounds and go on to be healers ourselves.

That question, "Why do some become healers and why do some become wounded wounders?" We will address that question throughout the book.

* * *

Today, I'm not preaching the 11 o'clock worship because as soon as I leave here, I'm heading to Edgefield, South Carolina, two and a half hours away. This is part of that story. A Black man 18 years of age picks up a pistol with two cousins and robs a store. Eddie Woods is given 7 years for armed robbery. Seven years in the South Carolina State Penitentiary. At the end of those seven years he finds the healer of his wounds, Jesus the Christ. He comes out only to find unemployment, rejection, alienation, almost to the point of picking up another gun several times. But then he begins to deal with a call to preach. He struggles for many years then comes to me in the Clinical Pastoral Education program at Kershaw prison. Three years he was with me and in those three years

---

[7] Arberry, A.J. The Koran Interpreted. New York, Simon & Schuster, 1955, p. 22.

dramatic healing took place. He wrote a little book, "Turning Points." Many of you have met him as he gave his testimony here. Today at 2 o'clock in Edgefield at Trinity Community Church, a dead AME congregation that Eddie has brought back to life as a community church, I'll be preaching his installation service. And probably while you are enjoying your dinner I'll still be enjoying their worship service. Eddie is part of and is an extension of you, who financially contributed to his life of healing as he is a healer to many others.

Because of my credentials, I have to have 40 hours a year of continuing education. About 3 years ago I selected a class in Charleston on woundedness. I'd never heard of Douglas C. Smith who was the workshop leader but I liked the title, so I attended the workshop. I wrote down a paragraph that Douglas C. Smith shared in that workshop. He is one of the finest workshops leaders I've ever heard. This is what he said, and I quote. *"In my childhood, I was continually moving from one home to another, having lived in over 15 places of residence before I was 15 years of age, never being able to establish any stable friendships. I know something about the woundedness of feeling friendless. When I came to my teenage years I graduated from high school with a 1.5 grade point average. That's a D+. I know some things about the woundedness of feeling mentally inadequate. Before reaching my mid-twenties I had lost my first child to death and before reaching my mid-thirties I had lost my youngest brother to death. I know something about woundedness of loosing a loved one. At age 38 I was institutionalized in a mental hospital. I know some things about the woundedness of feeling emotionally and psychologically inadequate. While in the mental hospital I was asked to renounce my priesthood in the Episcopal Church after being ordained for 14 years. I know some things about the woundedness of losing a sense of purpose and one's vocation. By age 40 I had experienced divorce. I know some things about the woundedness of going through a divorce and unwanted separation from one's children. Now, as I begin my fifth decade, I have increasing physical problems - one of a continual physical tremor that causes me to shake uncontrollably. I know something about the woundedness of social embarrassment."* [8]

---

[8] Smith, Douglas C. Being A wounded Healer. Madison, Wisconsin, Psycho-Spiritual Publications, 1999, p. 16.

9

Conclusion

The medical and the psychological model would say to Douglas C. Smith, "You are deeply, deeply sick and need to be on medication and in treatment." But the wounded healer model says, "You are in a place to live as a compassionate caring healer in a way that many other people cannot." We need not be overcome by our wounds. We need not perpetuate our own wounds onto others through brutality - verbal abuse or physical abuse. There is healing in our Christ who loved us so much that he became the supreme model of a wounded healer.

This morning as I was coming here from the church, I saw a squirrel right in the middle of my lane of traffic. His little feet felt the vibration of my vehicle and his little ears heard the roar of my engine. He runs to the right, and then to the left, and then to the right, and then he turns down the middle and I went right over him. The truck just went right over him. The tires didn't touch him. I looked in my rearview mirror as he made it to the grass. I could hear him say, "Wow! I should have made up my mind quicker!"

I pray that you will make up your mind this morning, because you like everyone here and like this speaker we are wounded. And I pray that we will decide this morning, this first worship service that I choose God's grace and God's forgiveness, I choose not to be a wounded wounder but a wounded healer. Decide today.

Let us pray.

Lord Jesus, we are amazed that one could be treated so brutally, even sacrificed in a criminal fashion, and yet become the world's preeminent wounded healer. All of us this morning stand in need of your healing. All of us this morning have been and are being wounded. Help us today to choose out of our woundedness to become healers. May it be so. In Jesus' name. Amen.

God bless you and keep you in his healing love. God bless you.

WHAT HAPPENS TO US IS NOT THAT IMPORTANT.

**IT IS WHAT HAPPENS TO WHAT HAPPENS
TO US THAT IS IMPORTANT.**

Abraham Lincoln (February 12, 1809-April 15, 1865) was America's 16th president. Lincoln's first wound was receiving less than twelve months of formal education in his formative years. His mother died when he was only nine years of age. Lincoln's older sister, Sarah, died in childbirth at age twenty in 1828. His first love, Ann Rutledge, died from typhoid fever (1835) before they were married. In 1842 he married Mary Todd. The couple had four sons with only one reaching adulthood. He was wounded by major depression throughout his lifetime. Yet, he began the healing of the nation issuing the "Emancipation Proclamation" in 1863. Although racial disparity continues, the healing began with this great healer.

(Carl Sandburg's Abraham Lincoln – A definitive six-volume work.)

DO YOU KNOW A WOUNDED HEALER?

CHAPTER 2

A PROPHECY OF THE WOUNDED

Text: Isaiah 53:1-12

CIT: Isaiah prophesied that the "Arm of God" (Jesus) would be
               wounded for humanity's wounds and through His suffering
               humanity would be healed.

Thesis: Through Jesus' wounds, we are healed.

Purpose:
               • Major Objective: Evangelistic
               • Specific Objective: Through the power of the Holy Spirit,
                 I hope to lead each of us in acceptance of God's healing.

Introduction

Outline:
   I.   Jesus' Wounds - vs. 3-11
        Despised (2) – Rejected – Sorrows (2) – Suffering (3) –
        Infirmities – Stricken (2) -Smitten (3)- Pierced - Crushed
        (2) - Punished - Wounds - Oppressed (2) - Afflicted (2)
   II.   Humanity's Healing - vs 4-6, 10-12
        "By His Wounds We Are Healed"

Conclusion: "He Himself bore our sins in his body on the tree, so that we
               might die to sins and live for righteousness: by his wounds
               you have been healed." (I Peter 2:24)

"I don't think
I could have ever been spiritually
redeemed had I not been
socially redeemed first."
~ Gene Rollins

The Word of the Lord

Isaiah 53: 1-12

1 Who has believed our message and to whom has the Arm of the Lord been revealed? 2 He grew up before him like a tender shoot and like a root out of dry ground. He had no beauty or majesty to attract us to him, nothing in his appearance that we should desire him. 3 He was despised and rejected by men. A man of sorrows and familiar with suffering like one from whom men hide their faces. He was despised and we esteemed him not.

4 Surely he took our infirmities and carried our sorrows. Yet we considered him stricken by God. Smitten by him and afflicted but he was pierced for our transgressions. 5 He was crushed for our iniquities. The punishment that brought us peace was upon him and by his wounds we are healed. 6 We all like sheep have gone astray. Each of us has turned to his own way and the Lord has laid on him the iniquity of us all.

7 He was oppressed and afflicted yet he did not open his mouth. He was led like a lamb to the slaughter and as a sheep before his shearer, he is silent. So he did not open his mouth. 8 By oppression and judgment he was taken away. And who can speak of his descendants for he was cut off from the land of the living. For the transgression of my people he was stricken. 9 He was assigned a grave with the wicked and with the rich in his death though he had done no violence nor was any deceit found in his mouth.

10 Yet it was the Lord's will to crush him and cause him to suffer and though the Lord makes his life a guilt offering he will see his offspring and prolong his days and the will of the Lord will prosper in his hand. 11 After the suffering of his soul he will see the light of life and be satisfied by his knowledge. My righteous servant will justify many and he will hear. He will bear their iniquities. 12 Therefore, I will give him a portion among the great and he will divide the spoils and with the strong because he poured out his life unto death and was numbered with the transgressors. For he bore the sin of many and made intercession for the transgressors..

Introduction

The beginning phrase, The Arm of God, The Arm of the Lord, arrested my attention in preparation. Isaiah uses that term in verses 51;5, 53:1, 62:8 and 63:12. I went to my biblical computer program, put in that phrase and the occurrence from scripture and from my commentary sources had 39551 hits. I thought I may as well stop the research right here. But it is a fascinating statement. Isaiah says the Arm of the Lord will redeem, reach down to you. As I thought about that phrase, it's personal. The Arm of the Lord reaches down in many ways through many different people.

I was 15 years of age, a deeply wounded and troubled adolescent. I had already been jailed twice. Quit school. I was hitchhiking to Spartanburg, SC and Broadus R. Littlejohn in a 1953 Desoto picked me up. One of his first questions was, "Son, why aren't you in school?" I said, "I quit." He said, "Well, what did your daddy think about that?" I said, "He's dead." Smart alec!

When I got out of the car the old man said to me as he slid his liver-spotted hand across the seat, "Son, if you're not going to go to school, come to the warehouse and talk to us. I'll give you a job." I knew he wouldn't. All I'd ever been able to get was part-time, piecemeal kinds of work. I was just 15. So, I really went to his office just to make a liar out of the old man. I went in and talked to Edgar Lancaster, the HR director. He told me what I knew he'd tell me. He said as he looked at my application, "Gene, if you'll come back when your 16, I'll talk to you about a job." I said, "Mr. Littlejohn said he would give me a job if I came by." He said, "Well, wait a minute."

Edgar walked down the hall and came back with Mr. Littlejohn. The old man stuck out his hand and said, "Gene, thank you for coming by." I could not believe the old man even remembered my name. He looked at Edgar and said, "Edgar, give him a job." Edgar looked funny but did the necessary paperwork.

Mr. Littlejohn had just broken the child labor law. But I found out through my many years with him, the law didn't mean a whole lot to him. Care and compassion meant everything to him. Had the Arm of the Lord not reached down through that man and redeemed me socially,

I don't know where I would be today if that had not happened. I have an idea. I don't think I could have ever been spiritually redeemed had I not been socially redeemed first.

Take a moment and think of the Arm of the Lord that has reached down in your life. For many different people, through many different experiences, think about those times your life has been touched, radically changed and/or healed through the Arm of the Lord coming in so many unexpected ways and persons.

Isaiah, writing 700 years before Jesus's birth, gets very specific about this Arm of the Lord. One can easily read that Isaiah is talking about a person, and not just any person. From chapter 40 all the way through chapter 66, the suffering servant is prophesied in varied and sundry ways. In this passage it is the central focus of those chapters 40 through 60.

Warren Wiersbe says this chapter is the Mount Everest of Isaiah's prophecy. Isaiah is saying that there is a Healer coming and that healer will bear our wounds, will carry our burdens, will take our transgressions. Very, very specific.[9]

Israel had the background to understand this passage so well. In the 18th chapter of Leviticus the writer introduces us to that day of Atonement and how what is called the scapegoat is a central focus of that day of Atonement. For it was that day and that day only that the high priest went beyond the curtain into the Holy of Holies. That place was considered so holy that they tied a rope around the High Priest's ankle in case he died back there. They have a bell on the other ankle. If the bell stopped ringing for a period of time, they did not go get him. That place was so holy they just took the rope and drug him out. But, before the High Priest went into that Holy place, they brought a goat known as the 'scapegoat.' Now, we've kind of lost that term. We just call it 'throwing me under the bus.' But they both have the same meaning.

The scapegoat would be taken before the people and the priest would put his hands on the head of the goat and confess the sins of his community, Israel, and confess his own sins. They would have a second goat. The second goat would be sacrificed on the altar and the goat that was the scapegoat would be taken out into the wilderness in a very

---

[9] http://www.sermoncentral.sermonid=145211

distant and desolate place called Azel, the place of demons. There the goat would be set free. It would symbolically carry the sins of the people away from them, outside the camp into the wilderness. So, Israel had a historical background to understand what Isaiah was saying, that there is one coming who will be stricken, smitten, pierced for you and for me.

The words you see in the Sermon Syllabus - all of them - are chosen so very, very carefully. We could spend several Sundays just looking at these words. I'm only going to pick out one that will give you an example. Pierced is "Chalal" in the Hebrew and it means a piercing so fierce and so hostel and with such degree, that the person Chalal is dead. The Hebrew does not have a stronger word to be used for the horrific piercing that would take place. It is true for all of the words that are in this section. Note them: despised, rejected, sorrows (twice), suffering (three times), infirmities, stricken (twice), smitten, pierced, crushed, wounded, oppressed, afflicted. Isaiah just goes on and on to describe these horrific wounds that Jesus would experience, prophesied 700 years before his birth. Jesus our Christ takes your sins and mine and our transgressions upon himself upon the tree.

There is the Arm of the Lord. Jesus the Christ, in a remarkable fashion, who came among us, lived sinless, compassionate, was a Healer in his life and a Healer for the world in his death.

As a very young preacher I met a Jewish evangelist named Hymen Appleman. I only heard him once. He's now dead but in that one hearing I heard him say this. He said, "You could have dangled me over hell forever and I would not have been remorseful. I would not have repented. I would not have changed. I would not have believed your suffering servant. But, when you dangle me over this passage, that is so clear about what the Lord did for me. I am not a dog. I could do nothing else other than accept personally his suffering for my death, his wounds for my healing." Wow! I don't know how many years ago I heard him say that but it has impacted me. I could identify with him. At the time of my conversion I was so hostile, angry, and aggressive that to threatened me by throwing me into Hell would have just given me the challenge of my lifetime. But confronted with this awesome love of God in Christ Jesus, how can one say no? How can one say no?

In Disney World there was an occurrence. It was time for Cinderella to make her appearance. All the little children were excited and gathered around waiting for her. She appeared and did perfect justice to that story of Cinderella. The young woman was absolutely flawless, beautiful in every way. She was standing in the midst of a sea of boys and girls wanting to touch her and be touched by her, be spoken to and to speak to. Except there was one little boy way over on the side holding the hand of his older brother. Deformed in stature, deformed in face, he had probably suffered enough rejection that he was not willing to step in and suffer another rejection. He stands by himself with his brother just watching this beautiful Cinderella. She very deliberately makes her way through that sea of children, gently talking to them, touching them, letting them touch her as she moved in the direction of that horribly deformed looking little creature. As she got to him, she knelt on her knees becoming eye level. She put her hands on both of his deformed cheeks and kissed several times his little ugly deformed face. Was that the Arm of the Lord for him? Was his little heart changed? I would imagine so. That's just what Jesus has done for us. That's what he's done for you.

Notice what the scripture says in verse 5, "…by his wounds we are healed." Not will be. Not have been. But, we are healed. The conclusion statement in 1 Peter 2:24 we read, "He himself bore our sins in his body on the tree so that we might die to sins and live for righteousness; by his wounds you have been healed."

1 John 2:2 says, "Jesus is the atoning sacrifice for our sins, and not only for ours but also for the sins of the whole world."

The few times I've been to New York I've thought of that verse when I came by the RCA building and saw this straining Atlas with the world on his shoulders. Not for our sins only but for the sins of the whole world, the scripture says. You have been healed. Can you hear the words? You have been healed.

Conclusion

Many years ago I was talking to a little group of boys at a youth camp. I reached in my wallet and pulled out a dollar bill. I said to the little boys, (there must have been 60 of them), "I want to give you this dollar." I was walking back and forth in front of them and I said this dollar is yours. It belongs to you." They just looked at me. I said, "This dollar yours?" And, they said, "Yeah." I said then, "Why is it still in my hand?" About that time little Butch on the front row, before anybody else could think about getting up and getting that dollar, was in front of me snatching that dollar out of my hand. I said, "See, it was not yours until you received it."

Have you received the Healing? Have you taken your wounds to the wounded one of prophecy who says, "I bore your iniquity. By my stripes you are healed." Have you?

Have you taken that promise and made it personal to your life? Therein is the source of us becoming healers to others. Our own wounds are healed. The way in which they are healed is through the wounds of our divine healer.

If I could, I would come sit beside you for just a moment and ask you if you've not received personally the healing of the wounded Lord Jesus, what is standing in your way? What keeps you from reaching out and taking that for yourself. "Through his stripes we are healed."

Let us pray.

Oh Lord, thank you for realizing many years ago that we were incapable of keeping the law. We were incapable because of our wounds. Thank you for loving us so much that you came as one of us, lived among us an exemplary life, a compassionate healing life and then died not for your criminal acts but for our transgressions. Lord, help each of us this morning to reach out and receive in faith the Grace of your healing upon us today. May it be so. In Jesus' name. Amen.

May God bless you and keep you. Keep you receiving the healing of Our Lord. God bless you.

WHAT HAPPENS TO US IS NOT THAT IMPORTANT.

IT IS WHAT HAPPENS TO WHAT HAPPENS TO US THAT IS IMPORTANT.

The pedagogical foundation of all learning is repetition.

In finding the place of our shared woundedness, and in respecting that place, respecting everyone's unique form of that mutual woundedness, we will open ourselves up to share in our mutual strengths and mutual healing. As Albert Kreinheder has said, "The greatest treasure comes out of the despised and secret places… This place of greatest vulnerability is also a holy place, a place of healing."

Kreinheder, A. (1991). <u>Body And Soul: The Other Side Of Illness.</u> Toronto: Inner City Books.

CHAPTER 3

ALL OF US ARE WOUNDED

Text: Psalm 36:1-4; Romans 3:10-20

CIT: *(Central Idea of the text)*
       All of Humanity has been wounded by sin.

Thesis: The human predicament is that all of humankind is wounded.

Purpose:

- Major Objective: Evangelistic
- Specific Objective: Through the power of the Holy Spirit, I hope to lead each of us in owning and confessing our woundedness.

Introduction

Outline:
   I.   Wounded in Character - Romans 3:12
   II.   Wounded in Conscience - vs10-11
   III. Wounded in Conversation - vs. 1-14
   IV.   Wounded in Conduct - vs. 15-18

Conclusion: "What shall we conclude then? Are we any better? Not at all!...All alike are under Sin." (Romans 3:9)

"The chance of life has wounded me.
My own stupid decisions
have wounded me.
...I am responsible.
I am 100% responsible
for everything I say,
do, and
think out of that woundedness."

The Word of the Lord

Psalm 36:1–4

1 An oracle is within my heart concerning the sinfulness of the wicked: There is no fear of God before his eyes.

2 For in his own eyes he flatters himself too much to detect or hate his sin.

3 The words of his mouth are wicked and deceitful; he has ceased to be wise and to do good.

4 Even on his bed he plots evil; he commits himself to a sinful course and does not reject what is wrong.

Romans 3:10–20

10 As it is written: "There is no one righteous, not even one; 11 there is no one who understands, no one who seeks God.

12 All have turned away, they have together become worthless; there is no one who does good, not even one.

13 Their throats are open graves; their tongues practice deceit. The poison of vipers is on their lips.

14 Their mouths are full of cursing and bitterness.

15 Their feet are swift to shed blood;

16 ruin and misery mark their ways,

17 and the way of peace they do not know.

18 There is no fear of God before their eyes."

19 Now we know that whatever the law says, it says to those who are under the law so that every mouth may be silenced and the whole world held accountable to God. 20 Therefore, no one will be declared righteous in his sight by observing the law; rather, through the law we become conscious of sin.

Introduction

I want to caution you that what I am presenting to you today is not Presbyterian theology. It is not even Orthodox theology. It is not good Orthodox Roman Catholic theology. You could say it's just Gene Rollins' theology. I have never asked you to agree with me on anything.

Never! Nor will I. But I do ask you to struggle to understand why I take some of the positions that I take. And, if you would like to further ferret out this position, the first two chapters in "The Mask" book describes pretty clearly my understanding of the nature and destiny of humankind. I put enough in those two chapters to be excommunicated from the Presbyterian Church. Hopefully they won't read it. There's enough in there to simply disbar me forever. And, that's okay. I was foolish or arrogant or stupid enough to put it in print. [10]

All of us are wounded. What I am <u>not</u> saying is that we are wounded in the classical way which classical theologians over the centuries have told us how we are wounded. I do not believe in original sin. I do not believe in a literal Fall in The Garden of Eden.

Charles Hodge, who was the primary spokesman for the fundamentalist position for many, many years, defines as clearly as I could find anywhere what the original sin means. By the way, that term is not in Scripture. That term was coined by Augustine in the year 354 and made into a big to-do out of Pauline theology. Here's what Charles Hodge said. (1) "All humankind descending from Adam is destitute of righteousness. (2) This original corruption affects his whole person - body, soul and spirit. (3) Fallen humankind is utterly indisposed, disabled and opposed to all that is good." That's what original sin means. But, since Adam, the first man (he takes that literally) and Eve were born, every person born since Adam and Eve is incurably depraved and totally depraved, unable to do any good. [11]

I have three major problems with that. First, if that is my condition, if because being human I am under the curse of Adam's sin, guilt and inability to do good then I am not responsible. I'm just being a child of Adam. You cannot hold me responsible for something I cannot help! I am amazed that people do not stand before judges and lawyers and say, "I'm not guilty. It was not me that did this. It was Adam who lives in me. You can not hold me accountable for something I can not prevent. I'm a sinner because I'm Adam's child, so don't hold me responsible." Do

[10] Rollins, Eugene C. The Masks We Wear. Bloomington, IN: Author House 2010, pp 1-20
[11] Hodge, Charles. Systematic Theology. Oak Harbor, WA: Logos, Inc. Research Systems. 1997

Wounded Wounder or Wounded Healer

you understand that? If I have no choice, I am a sinner simply because I was born.

The number 2 problem that I have with that: That being true, I cannot then choose to be a Healer. If I am wounded in that fashion, not by any choice of mine, then I cannot choose to do good. I cannot choose to be helpful to humanity. I cannot choose.

The basic passage that you see referenced in every commentary I pick up in relationship to Original Sin, is the 51st chapter of Psalm, verse 5 wherein David says, "In sin, my mother conceived me." We don't know who David's mother was. They didn't name women back then just like they didn't name their cows or anything else that they owned. David's father was named Jesse but he was married to David's mother whatever she was named. When you literalize lines in that passage you were saying that the marital bed is sinful and any product of that marital bed is degenerate and sinful.[12] It does not harmonize with the text in Hebrews that says the marriage bed is Holy and undefiled. And, what it also says, if you take that passage literally, that precious little boy sitting in that crib is a reprobate. He was born in sin. He cannot do anything in his life but sin. Can you see me taking that little boy walking out into that water and holding him up and saying, "Thank God for this little bundle of sin?" I may as well dunk him in the water and leave him out there. The Psalmist says, the Lord giveth and the Lord taketh away. Blessed be the name of the Lord. He doesn't have a chance. What I have a problem with is that we know full well what self-fulfillment prophecy means. You tell this little child he's a reprobate, he's a sinner, all he can do is bad things and sin, what's he going to do? Hello! What's he going to do? He's going to sin. Why not tell him he's a blessed creation of God. He is a spirit created in the image of God.

A child psychiatrist was asked why Jesus was such a marvelous person. She said in answer to that question, "Because he was told he was God's child." Well, Preacher, if you say all are wounded, if you agree with these texts of scripture, then aren't you saying the same thing? No.[13]

In 1941, Reinhold Niebuhr wrote that classic, The Nature and

---

[12] Hebrews 13:4
[13] Fox, Matthew, Speech in Ashville, NC 1984.

27

Destiny of Man. He said this and he was scandalized for it, "The Christian doctrine of original sin in its classic form offends the rationalists and the moralists alike." [14]

Walter Rauschenbusch later wrote, "Theology has done considerable harm in concentrating the attention of religious minds on the biological transmission of sin and evil." [15]

I believe both those statements. Here's what I believe. Humankind was created a dialectical Spirit creature. A dialectical is something that by its very essence is in tension. We were created not good or not evil. We were created in the image of God as dialectical creatures living in this tension of being the creature that we are and being the spirit that we are. And, in that we become wounded. Wounded by life itself. Wounded by our choices. Wounded by the choices of others, and, not being a good Presbyterian, wounded by chance. There are times when you're just in the wrong place at the wrong time. Life wounds us all. Everyone of us. And we are wounded, and it is my choice of that word to describe what sin is. Our world does it to us. I confess that I am wounded and life itself is wounding. Many other people have wounded me. The chance of life has wounded me. My own stupid decisions have wounded me. Then I am responsible. I am 100% responsible for everything I say, do, think out of that woundedness. I can't blame Adam, nor mama, nor anyone else. It's me, it's me, oh God, standing in the need of prayer. But we are wounded. We are wounded in character.

Listen to what the scripture says: "All have turned away. They have all together become worthless. There is no one who does good, not even one." (Romans 3:12) All of us were wounded in character in so many different ways.

The 28th president (1913-1921) of the United States, Woodrow Wilson, was a man I think all presidential historians agree was worthless. He was a poor president. The worst character wound he had was no one could tell him anything. No one. The only aide that he had that ever got anywhere with him was an aide by the name of House.

---

[14] Niebuhr, Reinhold. The Nature and Destiny of Man. New York: Charles Scribner's Sons. 1941, p. 241

[15] Rauschenbusch, Walter. A Theology for the Social Gospel. New York: The MacMillan Company. 1917, p. 67

Colonel House would always slip it in the back door. He would plant the seed and then let President Wilson act like it was his own thought. But Woodrow Wilson was so wounded by his fundamental Presbyterian preacher father, that he carried those wounds of character all of his life. We are wounded, all of us. Some physical diseases can turn us inside out. We're wounded by emotional, mental diseases that wreck havoc with our lives. All of us are wounded. Our consciences are wounded.[16]

Listen to what the scripture says. "It is written there is no one righteous, not even one. No one who understands. No one who seeks God." (Roman 3:10-11)

In 1984, I was a teaching chaplain at Marsh Village Addiction Center, Department of South Carolina Mental Health. I developed a unique rapport with this young man who was addicted. I developed his trust and he told me this story. He said, "On a Saturday afternoon I was driving down the highway and I saw two Mexican wetbacks (his term) on the side of the road. I pulled over behind them. I hit the first one with a tire tool. Then, I began carving on the other one with my pocket knife. Then, I began carving on the one that was lying on the ground unconscious."

I said, "Why in the world did you do that? What had they done to you?"

"I didn't know them. They were wetbacks. They have no right to be here. They have no right at all."

I was just stunned. In those days it was our legal responsibility to put everything about our conversations with these patients in their medical chart. So, I charted this conversation. A week or so later he was hurt playing basketball on the court at Marsh Village. They came and got me to take him to Burns Clinic. They gave me his medical chart and I loaded him up and took him there. I was shaking like a leaf inside all the way there, but it was worse coming back. I took him in the clinic and took his chart to the doctor. I introduce them and told him the situation and he sat down. The doctor sat down beside him in a little waiting area and I was called back to do some paperwork. I left. The doctor had his chart in his hand. I came back after a few minutes. The doctor was gone and my patient was sitting there reading his own medical chart.

---

[16] Bits and Pieces, Nov. 1975, p. 6

He said to me with some of the coldest eyes I've ever looked into, "You wrote about me in that chart."

Oh my goodness. I had to ride home with this guy. Well, I had sense enough to call for reinforcements. Several of us rode home with him. I had sense enough to get him another therapist as well.

This person had no remorse whatsoever about carving up these two human men. None. I don't even think I need to go into illustrating the next two about how our conversation and our conduct is wounded. "Their throats are open graves, their tongues practice deceit. The poison of vipers is on their lips. Their mouths are full of cursing and bitterness. Their feet are swift to shed blood; ruin and misery mark their ways and the way of peace they do not know. There is no fear of God before their eyes." (Romans 3:13-18) I don't even think I need to illustrate that. I think all you need to do is think of your relationships. Think of your experiences and the conversation and the conduct that you've experienced as being deeply, deeply wounded.

A missionary was in ministry in Brazil and at one of his meetings, a mother came to him and asked him if he would go to the local prison and visit her youngest son? He agreed. Upon visiting the son he found a deeply distraught, depressed, wounded young man. And, presenting him with the Forgiveness of God, the young man said, "I cannot be forgiven. I must die for my sins. I have shed blood. I must have my blood shed. I killed my wife and my unborn child. The missionary did not dissuade him from the seriousness of his admission to that horrible act. But the missionary shared with him Isaiah 53:5. He, Jesus, was wounded. He, Jesus, shed his blood for your transgressions; and, with his stripes, with his shedding of blood, you are healed.

When we understand our sin in this world it is because of our own woundedness and contribution to the woundedness of our society. When we stop blaming it on some mythic figure who lived thousands of years ago, and accept that I am responsible for my sin in my woundedness and what I do with it, then we may be able to get somewhere in this country.

Pierce Harris for many years was minister of the First Methodist Church in Atlanta, Georgia. He was a fabulous preacher. He went to a prison in Atlanta to speak on an occasion. An inmate introduced Dr. Harris. At the conclusion of his introduction, the inmate said, "Two young boys grew up, rough on the streets of downtown Atlanta. Those two boys went to Sunday School together. One of those boys dropped out; one of them stayed. The one who introduces our speaker today is the one who dropped out. Our speaker today is the one who stayed." That's responsibility.

Conclusion

We are wounded by many sources. It is my choice with God's help, whether or not I'm going to wallow in my wounds in anger, hostility, revenge and be a wounded wounder or if I am going to accept the fact that I am wounded and some of my woundedness is by my own choices. What can I do with it? How can I find healing in Jesus the Christ whose stripes were there for me? How can I accept that forgiveness and healing, and then commit my life to becoming a healer of others? It's up to you. It's up to me. It's up to you and you. Enough of blaming it on Adam. Let us embrace the responsibility. I am what I am because of me and my woundedness. Now what do I do with it? It is your choice.

Let us pray:

Lord Jesus, thank you so much for your willingness to become one of us, live among us, and experience your wounds of rejection, ridicule, physical punishment, and death. All for us. Help us to hear and to know that you are our ultimate wounded healer. If we accept your healing, we, too, can become healers. In Jesus' name, may it be so. Amen.

May God bless you and keep you healing in your wounds and healing others. God bless you.

WHAT HAPPENS TO US IS NOT THAT IMPORTANT.

IT IS WHAT HAPPENS TO WHAT HAPPENS TO US THAT IS IMPORTANT.

2019 Time's Person of the Year

Greta Thunberg of Stockholm, Sweden was wounded by a birth defect called Asperger Syndrome. At age 11. She was wounded by a deep depression that she called "an endless sadness." Yet, she has become the number one healer of our planet inspiring millions of people across more than 150 countries. Because of her, more than 60 nations have agreed to have net carbon footprint of zero by the year 2050.

(Time, December 23-30, 2019)

CHAPTER 4

JACOB: WOUNDED BY GOD

Text: Genesis 32:22-32

CIT: *(Central Idea of the text)*
          A Manifestation of God wrestled with Jacob all night and wounded him in such a way that Jacob was never the same again.

Thesis: When we are wounded by God's touch we will never be the same again.

Purpose:
     • Major Objective: Evangelistic
     • Specific Objective: Through the power of the Holy Spirit, I hope to lead each of us in allowing God to touch us deeply.

Introduction

Outline:
    I.   The Travail – vs. 22-24
    II.   The Triumph - vs. 25-27
   III. The Transformation - vs. 28-29
   IV. The Testimony - vs. 30-32

Conclusion: "So Jacob called the place Peniel, saying it is because I saw God face to face..." (Genesis 32:30)

"Anger boiled up in me.
When you can be
angry at the
Highest Authority,
you can be angry
at any lesser authority:
policemen,
school teachers.
It doesn't matter."

The Word of the Lord

Genesis 32:22–32

22 That night Jacob got up and took his two wives, his two maidservants and his eleven sons and crossed the ford of the Jabbok. 23 After he had sent them across the stream, he sent over all his possessions. 24 So Jacob was left alone, and a man wrestled with him till daybreak. 25 When the man saw that he could not overpower him, he touched the socket of Jacob's hip so that his hip was wrenched as he wrestled the man.

26 Then the man said, "Let me go, for it is daybreak." But Jacob replied, "I will not let you go unless you bless me."

27 The man asked him, "What is your name?" "Jacob," he answered.

28 Then the man said, "Your name will no longer be Jacob, but Israel, because you have struggled with God and with men and have overcome."

29 Jacob said, "Please tell me your name." But he replied, "Why do you ask my name?" Then he blessed him there.

30 So Jacob called the place Peniel, saying, "It is because I saw God face to face, and yet my life was spared."

31 The sun rose above him as he passed Peniel, and he was limping because of his hip.

32 Therefore to this day the Israelites do not eat the tendon attached to the socket of the hip, because the socket of Jacob's hip was touched near the tendon.

Introduction

The sermon this morning has caused me more anxiety than any sermon I will preach this summer. The very title of it is anxiety-producing and perplexing. So if you will please give me 10 minutes and then after the 10 minutes you can drift off and watch the lake and look for the eagle and plan your dinner or whatever else that you do while I'm preaching. But please give me 10 minutes.

God does not wound us physically. Hear that. I would not wish upon anyone what I went through for fifteen years. I watched my father die when he was age 42 and I was four. He died with a massive heart attack right in front of us. I grew up believing that God killed my father. We were thrown into horrific poverty and of course that was God's fault as well since we had no provider. Most of the time Mama was too ill with black lung disease to work. We primarily fended for ourselves. Anger boiled up in me. When you can be angry at the highest authority, you can be angry at any lesser authority: policeman, school teachers. It doesn't matter. And I spent those years as one hostile angry youth. And it got me into all kinds of trouble.

Things began to change when I said to Aunt Sally, "God killed my daddy." And she grabbed me and shook me and said, "God had nothing to do with your daddy's death. Your daddy died with a heart attack, heart disease, just like my husband Burnes did, and his other brother Dennis did, and his daddy Matt did when he was 56. Son, get that foolishness out of your head. He died with heart disease."

It is not God that kills us! It is disease that kills us. How many other people have I dealt with throughout my life who spend immense years of torment questioning and blaming God for what disease does. Think about it. The only way the people of scripture knew how to talk about it was that God caused everything.

A woman came to me several years ago, distraught and depressed. She said that her Pastor said to her when she and her husband visited the pastor with their little Down Syndrome child, "God selected you because you are precious, compassionate, caring parents to raise this child." When she said that to me I just wanted to scream. Who then in God's name would want to be a good parent? If I'm a good, caring, compassionate parent, then God's going to do something like that to me simply because I'm compassionate and caring? What kind of thinking is that? Who would want to be a good parent? God up in the sky says, "Okay, I got this little mentally retarded child and here's a wonderful parent and I have to meet my quota and give out mentally retarded children this month. So there. You got one." It's genes, folks. Its genetic. It's disease. How long is it going to take us in the "Age of Enlightenment" to come out of this kind of understanding?

George C. Patton was marching his army across Germany. Third Army. They got bogged down in snow. He called his chaplain and he said, "Chaplain, write me a prayer of good weather for tomorrow." And in the movie you can see the angst's on the chaplain's face. The chaplain said, "Okay. I'm going to write a prayer asking God for good weather so we can speedily go off and kill more people." You can just see the angst's on the chaplain face. And, of course General Patton said, "Do it!" And he did. That night Patton is out reading this beautiful prayer that the chaplain wrote. The next morning the sky cleared and there was no snow. And Patton said, "Bring that chaplain to me. I want to give him a medal."

The chaplain knew as I know that prayer didn't have anything to do with it. We know where the weather comes from. Our weathermen and women predict the weather.

Recently, I had an outside wedding. When I got there the sky was as black as a pit. I had a couple of people asked me about praying for the cloud to move away and not rain. I said okay. It cleared up. No rain. Great wedding outside.

We're headed home and my wife Linda said, "You didn't really pray that, did you?"

"Of course not! I didn't pray that. I've got many people living just below the area where we had the wedding praying for rain on their crops."

God does not wound us physically. God wounds us in our conscience. And that's precisely what he did in this magnificent story.

"Well, preacher, what about his hip? His hip was out of joint the rest of his life." Well it was according to the story. But the purpose of God manifesting God's self to Jacob was to wound his conscience because Jacob was a horribly wounded person, wounded at birth. The story is that when the twins Jacob and Esau were born, Esau was born first becoming the child of blessing or the first born. The story is that as Esau came out of the womb, Jacob had him by the heel trying to pull him back in. And, he lived out his name, that of Supplanter, Deceiver, Conniver all of his life.

Esau is out hunting. Jacob's a mama's little boy and stays home. Esau comes in famished and Jacob says to him, "I have some really nice stew and you can have some but it's going to cost you. I want your birthright."

And Esau says, "What good is a birthright. I'm about to starve to death." Jacob tricked him out of his birthright.

When it's time for the parental blessing upon the first born, Esau is again out hunting...my kind of man. Jacob fixes a great stew and brings it to his father. But before he does, his mother Rebecca - that's another way he was wounded; he was a spoiled child by his mama - Rebecca takes the skin of the goat and puts on Jacob's arm because his brother is hairy and Jacob is hairless and fair skinned. Jacob goes to his blind father with his soup, his meal, and his father says to him, "Wow, so quickly you found game." And, the little Deceiver says to him, "Your God has blessed me so with hunting success. Jacob feeds him and then his blind father blesses him with Esau's blessing.

Esau is so angered that Jacob leaves. Flees. Goes to his mother's and brother's place. She's still enabling the little Trickster. And it was there that he falls in love with Rachel and Laban says for him to work 7 years and he'll let Jacob have her. He worked 7 years. The scriptures tell us that he loved her so that those seven years were as if they were a day. Isn't that romantic? At the end of the seven years, Rachel being the youngest daughter, Laban gives him Leah the eldest daughter. So, they are at a wedding drinking, having a great time and he goes to bed with Rachel and wakes up with Leah. There's a lot of people that's done that folks. Lot of people have done that. Well, the Trickster is tricked by his father-in-law. He has to work seven more years but he does give him Rachel before the seven years. He gives him Rachel a week after he marries Leah.

But the Trickster continues. One little example. He says to his father-in-law, "I've been working, herding, and taking care of all your possessions. What about me?" So, Jacob says to him, "I'll make you this deal. I'll take care of all of our flocks if you will let me have the least desirable, the spotted ones, those that are blemished and not perfect. I'll take the ugly duckling." So, Laban agrees.

Jacob stables, corrals, pins all of the spotted ones, all of the blemished ones together. Do you realize what he just did? They knew nothing about genetics back in those days, but when you put spot to spot, the increase chances of giving birth to spot increases and this is precisely what the Trickster did and his flock multiplied.

In our texts he has now left. He's going back home. He is in deep travail. He does not know what Esau will do. Frightened, anxious, worried, he sends his family across the river and he stays alone. While alone God meets him. God manifests God's-self in the form of a person - probably an Angelic person. This person wrestles, physically wrestles. There are those who believe it's an allegory. I personally do not. It was no big thing for angels to appear in the Old Testament or New Testament. Jacob wrestles with this man/angel all night. Neither prevail. They continued the struggle and the angel says at daylight, "Let me go. It's daylight." Jacob says, "No. I'm not going to let you go until you bless me."

At some point, Jacob realizes what he's dealing with. There's one theologian who makes a strong case that this angel was Esau's Guardian Angel. And that Jacob's prevailing against Esau's Guardian Angel, truly earned him the right of the inheritance, the blessing. Maybe.

There are those who work very hard to make life just, which it never is. But the angel says to Jacob, "What's your name?" And, he says, "the Deceiver, Jacob the Trickster, the Supplanter."

And the angel says, "No longer. Your name will now be Israel."

When we meet God face to face and God wounds our conscience, our essence, it changes us. A human's essence in those days was represented by their name. "No longer will you be Trickster. You will be one who prevailed with God, struggled with God, and prevailed."

Jacob's life was changed. When God wounds us, God wounds us in our conscience for a purpose and that purpose is for us to see ourselves as we truly are. In that moment of recognition, realizing that God can make us what we are not, and it is in the struggle, this dynamic tension, that Jacob is triumphant and his testimony becomes, "I have met God face to face."

Have you met God face to face? Ever been at some point where God struggled with you on a conscience level and you knew you became aware of what you were and allowed God to touch you and change you?

Many years ago my second child came to the bedroom I was awakened by her standing by the bed crying. She was eight years of age. Awakened, I got out of bed and picked her up and held her until she quit snubbing and she said, "Daddy, I took Mary's pencil today at school and I still have it." Well, I knew this had a lot more to do than being about a pencil. For in her little life God had struggled with her and she realized she was not what God wanted her to be.

Have you met God? Has God touched your conscience? Have you allowed him to change your name?

Conclusion

James Cash Penny, originator of J.C. Penny in Missouri. ('Jacque Pennay' - that's where I get my clothes). In 1931 he went bankrupt. James Cash Penney lost over $40 million. In that financial wounding, he went to the State Mental Hospital deeply, deeply depressed. It was in the state hospital that he heard a church choir from the community which came and they began singing,

> *"Be not dismayed whate'er betide. God will take care of you.*
> *Beneath his wings of love abide through every day or all the way,*
> *God will take care of you."*

In that moment James Cash Penny was struggling with an angel that touched his conscience and his name didn't change but his life did. And, he has been a benevolent benefactor all of these years for the cause of Christ.

Has your conscience been touched? Have you struggled with what and who God wants you to be? May it be so.

Let us pray.

Lord, You who heals the brokenhearted and binds up their wounds, comfort the sick, the hungry, the lonely and those who hurt and shut-in on themselves, by your presence in their hearts use us to help them in a practical way. Show us how to set about this and give us strength, tact and compassion. Teach us how to be alongside them and how to share in their distress deeply in our prayers. Make us open to them and give us courage to suffer with them, that in so doing, we share with you in the suffering of the world for we are your body on Earth and you work through us. And Lord, if there are those here this morning who have not realized your touch upon their conscience, may they hear your voice; may they be open to the struggle this day. In Jesus' name. Amen.

May God bless you and keep you healing from your wounds. God bless you.

WHAT HAPPENS TO US IS NOT THAT IMPORTANT.

**IT IS WHAT HAPPENS TO WHAT HAPPENS
TO US THAT IS IMPORTANT.**

Rachel Naomi Remen has said, "It's our woundedness that allows us to trust each other. I can trust another person only if I can sense that they, too, have woundedness, have pain, have fear. Out of that trust we can begin to pay attention to our own wounds and to each other's wounds – and to heal and be healed."

Remen, R.N. (1993), "Wholeness" in Bill Moyers, <u>Healing And The Mind</u>. New York: Doubleday.

CHAPTER 5

JOB: WOUNDED BY EVIL

Text: Job 2:1-10

CIT: *(Central Idea of the text)*
              Job, a "perfect and upright" person was wounded by the
              "accuser."

Thesis: There is an evil force in our world which will wound us.

Purpose:
- Major Objective: Doctrinal
- Specific Objective: Through the power of the Holy Spirit,
  I hope to lead each of us in living alert to the evils of our
  world.

Introduction

Outline:
I.   Wounds Come to One and All - vs.1:1, 2:3
II.   Wounds Come From Material Loss - vs. 1:13-22
III. Wounds Come From Physical Loss - vs. 2:6-10
IV.   Wounds Come From Unknown Sources – vs. 38:1-42:9

Conclusion:

"I've looked into the eyes of murderers,
thieves,
rapists,
child molesters,
and I've never seen Satan.
What I have seen
in these faces and in these eyes
are souls, spirits, lives
that have been horribly wounded."

"...as long as we project
the responsibility
of our wounding
onto something
or someone
other than ourselves
we will be wounders
until we die
and some of us gleefully so."

"As long as
I look outward to whomever/whatever
made me do it,
I will not take inventory
of who and what I am,
nor where my wounds are
so that I might seek healing
and not continue to perpetuate
this evil onto other people."

The Word of the Lord

Job 2:1-10

1 On another day the angels came to present themselves before the LORD, and Satan also came with them to present himself before him. 2 And the LORD said to Satan, "Where have you come from?" Satan answered the LORD, "From roaming through the earth and going back and forth in it."

3 Then the LORD said to Satan, "Have you considered my servant Job? There is no one on earth like him; he is blameless and upright, a man who fears God and shuns evil. And he still maintains his integrity, though you incited me against him to ruin him without any reason."

4 "Skin for skin!" Satan replied. "A man will give all he has for his own life. 5 But stretch out your hand and strike his flesh and bones, and he will surely curse you to your face."

6 The LORD said to Satan, "Very well, then, he is in your hands; but you must spare his life."

7 So Satan went out from the presence of the LORD and afflicted Job with painful sores from the soles of his feet to the top of his head. 8 Then Job took a piece of broken pottery and scraped himself with it as he sat among the ashes.

9 His wife said to him, "Are you still holding on to your integrity? Curse God and die!"

10 He replied, "You are talking like a foolish woman. Shall we accept good from God, and not trouble?" In all this, Job did not sin in what he said.

Introduction

This message produces for me almost as much anxiety as the last message, Wounded by God. I realize there are some very deeply held beliefs about God and Satan. My conclusion in the last message, not necessarily yours because I don't ever ask that you agree, was that God does not wound us. God does not wound us in body and in mind. Disease does that. God wounds our conscience and always for the single purpose of bringing us to conviction that we might become better persons; persons more fully healed than before. That's what I believe about God.

Apparently, quite a few of you did not turn me off totally with that message because you're back this morning. So I'll take another jab at you.

I have looked into the face of evil and I did not see Satan. I've looked into the eyes of evil and I did not see the eyes of Satan. I've looked into the eyes of murderers, thieves, rapists, child molesters, and I've never seen Satan. What I have seen in these faces and in these eyes are souls, spirits, lives that have been horribly wounded. They have not gotten over those wounds. And they have perpetuated their wounds in life upon others as one great tragic evil. I'm not saying there's not a Satan simply because I've never seen it. I've never seen God but I believe God is.

CS Lewis in his little book "Screwtape Letters" said there are two cautions we need to have in relationship to Satan. He said, "I caution us not to disbelieve it and I caution us not too excessively believe it." [17] I've been with both those parties; I've been with people who prayed doorknob demons out of broken door knobs; flat tire demons out of flat tires. The whole world's like that. It's a cough demon, a pneumonia demon. Whatever it is, there is a 'Flip Wilson' in our world. "The devil made me do it." And any time I can take that stance I can do whatever I please and accept no responsibility. "The devil made me do it."

Before I give you the origin of this book and get into it a little deeper, let me caution you about taking the Book of Job literally, word for word. For when you do you really have some problems. Here's the first one. I'll illustrate. When our dog was about three, Wateree Will - we call him Ree - I developed a habit. I don't know why, but when I let him out at night to do his last bathroom call, I would leave the deck dark and I would open the door and say, "Get him!" He would tear out the door. He doesn't tear out much anymore because he's almost 11 years old. He's old like his daddy. On this particular night I opened the door and I said, "Get him!" Well he got it. I heard this awful commotion and by the time I could get the light on I saw Ree flip a raccoon all the

[17] Lewis, C.S. The Screwtape Letters and Screwtape Proposes a Toast. New York: The Macmillan Company. 1961. p. 3

way out onto the sidewalk. Poor raccoon hit the sidewalk and struggled off trying to get back to the woods and I called Ree off. I will never do that again. I just open the door and say, "Ease out boy."

If you literalize the book of Job, that's exactly what you have taking place. Satan comes before God and God says let me point someone out to you. His name is Job. He's perfect, righteous, upright and absolutely pure. "Get him. Sic him." Where's the motivation to live a good life? I don't want to be recognized by God as being good if God is going to say, "Sic him. Really see what he's made of." No, I'm going to flounder around making all kinds of willful mistakes, get into all kinds of stuff, do all kinds of bad things. I don't want to be labeled perfect, upright if God's going to say, "Sic him." Do you see what you do when you literalize this book?

There are some other problems, too. We didn't read the first attack. We read the second on his body. In the first attack he loses everything. All of his stock killed, all taken. His seven sons and his three daughters are having a feast and there is a great tornado. The house falls upon all 10 of them and killed them. Well, so be it. They are not central characters in it any way. They're just people. What kind of God is that? "I want to get Gene so I'm just going to kill his children." What about the children? What did they do? If you take the book literally then you got to answer those questions or do the ostrich syndrome - dig your head in the sand.

The book of Job originated - this is not my opinion; this is very serious valid research – the book of Job, probably the oldest written piece of the Old Testament, originated in Iraq which in the Bible is Babylon. Israel was taken captive into Iraq/Babylon and they were there about forty years and while there they became acquainted with this drama which was a play. It's interesting to me and a criticism of me which is okay. I don't have a problem with criticism except from my wife Linda. When you read the book of Job in Hebrew or the Book of Genesis, no one has to say to you that you are reading poetry because it is magnificently beautiful poetry. If you read a poem in English no one has to say to you that you are reading a poem. [18]

Martin Luther describes Job as magnificent and sublime. The

<hr>

[18] Jung, C.G. Answer to Job. New Jersey: Princeton University Press. 1958, p. 3

marvelous poet Tennyson called it the greatest poem of ancient or modern times. Carlisle said, "I call it one of the grandest things ever written. A noble book. All men's book. There is nothing written I think in the Bible or out of it equal in literary merit." C.F. Kant referred to the book of Job as the Matterhorn of the Old Testament. H. H. Riley said, "The Book of Job is the Supreme literary Masterpiece of poetry in the Old Testament and one of the greatest creations of the world's religions," and it's generally agreed.

The book of Job originated as a drama, a play to explain the popular theological understanding that if one is good, loves God, believes in God and tithes, then wonderful things are going to happen to you. If on the other hand you are a disbeliever, you do not love God then horrible things happened to you.

Read Psalms 1. That's what Psalms 1 is all about. Go home and read it. David cried out, "Why do the righteous suffer and the wicked prosper?" David's life experience did not jive with what the scriptures were saying and David is questioning. And, in the marvelous little classical book Why Do Good People Suffer, Rabbi Kushner struggled with this question in the premature death of his son. Why do good people suffer horribly at times? This question was the question of the day as it is the question of our day. This drama, this play developed and Israel liked it. When they returned the remnant of people, they took it with them.

However, it so cut at the heart of their understanding, they couldn't leave it as it ended. The book of Job in its original form did not have those last verses in it where Job has more children, more handsome, stronger than all the others, and more beautiful. He has more sheep, more cattle, has more of everything that he had before. Everything! That wasn't in the drama; that wasn't in the play. The drama, the play in its original form left you with that question, 'I do not know why good people suffer.' But we all do - good or bad.

Suffering is universal. Woundedness is universal. We are often wounded as Job was wounded when we lose things because we connect, bond to the material world as it should be. Many suicides took place in the great crash of the 1920's. To lose anything produces grief, heart hurt, innate pain, wounds.

Job had a horrible physical loss and in that physical loss he maintained his integrity. Not everyone does. A preacher in Lyman, South Carolina who had been a mentor of mine in the very earliest days of my ministry came down with lung cancer while I was in seminary in Texas. The pain, the agony, the prognosis became so futile and horrible, the wounds so deep and agonizing that he took his own life. My mama called me and wanted me to know from her because she felt like I'd be devastated, which I was not. Saddened, but I understood.

I do not see Satan roaming back and forth on the Earth inflicting pain and evil. What I see is wounded people who never healed, perpetuating their wounds upon others at times as if it is a right to do so.

I think it is a cop-out that will not help us one iota when we believe that there is some evil force outside myself that is going to control me and calls me to do things that are immoral, unethical or unhelpful to other people. I do not need to look outward. I need to look inward. As long as I look outward for whomever/whatever made me do it, I will not take inventory of who and what I am nor where my wounds are so that I might seek healing and not continue to perpetuate this evil on to other people.

How many times sitting in my office do I hear stories like, "Well, when she gets on me like she does, I just can't help it. Anger takes complete control of me." Whose fault is it? Of course you know whose fault it is. "It's her fault. She shouldn't get me that angry."

I said to a fella a couple years ago who was hitting on his wife, "Where do you work?" He told me. I said, "How long have you worked there?" He said, "17 years." I said, "So, you never got mad at work?" He said, "Yeah, I've got mad at work a lot of times." I said, "Who did you punch out?" He said, "I didn't punch out anybody. They would have fired me." I said, "Hello!"

As long as we are projecting the evil that we perpetrate onto something, someone outside of ourselves we will never be healed. You've heard of the 'Freudian slip,' "I didn't mean to say that." Freud said, "Oh, yes you did." "I was drunk. I didn't mean to say that." Oh, yes you did. "I was angry. I didn't mean to say that." Oh, yes you did. There is a part of you that wanted to say that or it would have never come out of your mouth. It was not because you were drunk, angry, mentally/emotionally upset. It's you. And it's me. And as long as we project the responsibility of our wounding onto something or someone other than ourselves we will be wounders until we die and some of us gleefully so.

We are all wounded in some way. I'm wounded. You're wounded. Job was wounded horribly by evil. The term for Satan is not used in Job. It is not a Hebrew word. It is in the Arabic word that we get the word accuser from. To translate that word Satan or devil is inaccurate. I know why they do it but it's inaccurate to do so. And we are accused, wounded through accusation by many people, in many situations, in many ways. The cause of evil in our world today is not Satanic. It is woundedness: human woundedness that will not be confessed, that will not be healed and that we continue to perpetuate.

I probably shouldn't quote this because it's not in our Bible. It is in the Catholic Bible. They have a section called the Apocrypha that is not in the Protestant Bible. But in the Catholic Bible in the book of Ecclesiasticus, I found this statement. Ecclesiastes 21:27, "When a bad man curses Satan, he is cursing himself." Wow! I think we probably took some stuff out we should have left in there. [19]

In the late fifties, early 60s after my conversion in 1961, I was exposed to a play written by Archibald MacLeish. The title of the play was JB, a take off from Job. The JB drama was current. JB was a wonderful, wonderful man, a delightful husband, delightful father, and a prominent business man, community-minded, civic directed. He was a Job. His eldest son is in the military and this is after the war is over and through a horrible mistake by his Commander, his son is killed. Two drunk GIs come to his house to tell him and his wife Sarah that their son has been killed. In the midst of that grief and horror, his two next children were in a car accident and they're both killed. Reeling and rocking from this, JB's youngest daughter and last child is raped and murdered. In the midst of this horrific loss Sarah leaves him. Unable to work, unable to function he is financially destitute. He has three friends that come and try to comfort him: a psychiatrist, which usually are no help; a counselor, they're usually no help either; and a priest, which is almost never any help. They weren't any help to JB. JB makes

---

[19] The New English Bible with the Apocrypha. Oxford University Press 1970, P. 145

a statement in that play that gripped me to the core of my being. JB said, "If God is good, God is not God and if God is God, God is not good." [20]

Conclusion

I'd like to leave you with that for a while. His closing statement was that the candles have gone out in the churches. The candles have gone out in the churches. The only candles that are burning are the candles within our heart - a totally humanistic conclusion, MacLeishe's JB. I'm not there but a lot of people are and I believe I know why a lot of people are there. It is the generations in our society who project all of the evil outside themselves. Until we come to "it is me, it is me, oh God, standing in the need of prayer," it is I who is wounded, my wounds aren't healed and I'm perpetuating those wounds onto others. Nothing, no one, no force outside myself caused me to do it. We need to stand flat-footed, look in the mirror, put on our big boy and girl panties, and say it is I. Quit looking somewhere else, finger pointing. Quit blaming. It is me, oh Lord, standing in the need of prayer. Jesus has given us a way. He said, "By my stripes you are healed, through my death you are freed. Through the transgressions you commit being placed upon me, you're set free to heal and to heal others." May it be so.

Let us pray.

Oh Lord, thank you for this magnificent piece of poetry, drama from old; for your inspiration that saved it for us and generations past and, yet, generations future. Help us to see the principal truth of this magnificent play, that horrible things happen to wonderfully good people. Good and bad, it is up to us to take our wounds. Own them. Confess them. Give them to you, and your suffering death and Resurrection, that we might be healed and then use our wounds and our healing to perpetuate healing upon others. Oh Lord, Jesus, may it be so. In Jesus' name, Amen.

May God bless you and keep you healing that you might be a healing to others. God bless you.

---

[20] MacLeish, Archibald. J. B. Boston: Houghton Mifflin Harcourt Publishing 1956, p14

WHAT HAPPENS TO US IS NOT THAT IMPORTANT.

**IT IS WHAT HAPPENS TO WHAT HAPPENS
TO US THAT IS IMPORTANT.**

Allow this statement to become your personal mantra.

The world is wounded. Every human experiences problems; no human escapes problems. We all have shortcomings; we all have imperfections. We all experience dissatisfaction. We are all confronted with adversity. We all share in the woundedness of the world. Yet, also, we can all experience healing in the midst of that woundedness, a healing that comes from facing the woundedness.

Smith, Douglas C. Being a Wounded Healer, Psycho-Spiritual Publications, Madison, Wisconsin (1999) p. 16

CHAPTER 6

CAIN: WOUNDED BY REJECTION

Text: Genesis 4:1-16

CIT: *(Central Idea of the text)*
              Cain suffered from the wound of rejection.

Thesis: All of us feel rejection from some source to some degree.

Purpose:
- Major Objective: Supportive
- Specific Objective: Through the power of the Holy Spirit, I hope to lead each of us in working through our rejection.

Introduction

Outline:
I.   Wounded By Seeing Acceptance - v. 4
II.   Wounded By Being Rejected - vs. 5-7
III. Wounds of Rejection Causes Homelessness - vs. 11-12
IV.   Wounds of Rejection Causes Fear of Being Found Out -vs. 14-16

Conclusion:

"When we are
so insecure
that we are driven
compulsorily
to live
pleasing everybody
in the world,
we set ourselves up for constant rejection."

"Our greatest Glory
is not in being never rejected
but our greatest glory
is in continuing
every time that we are."

The Word of the Lord

Genesis 4:1–16

1 Adam lay with his wife Eve, and she became pregnant and gave birth to Cain. She said, "With the help of the LORD I have brought forth a man." 2 Later she gave birth to his brother Abel. Now Abel kept flocks, and Cain worked the soil. 3 In the course of time Cain brought some of the fruits of the soil as an offering to the LORD. 4 But Abel brought fat portions from some of the firstborn of his flock. The LORD looked with favor on Abel and his offering, 5 but on Cain and his offering he did not look with favor. So Cain was very angry, and his face was downcast.

6 Then the LORD said to Cain, "Why are you angry? Why is your face downcast? 7 If you do what is right, will you not be accepted? But if you do not do what is right, sin is crouching at your door; it desires to have you, but you must master it."

8 Now Cain said to his brother Abel, "Let's go out to the field." And while they were in the field, Cain attacked his brother Abel and killed him.

9 Then the LORD said to Cain, "Where is your brother Abel?" "I don't know," he replied. "Am I my brother's keeper?"

10 The Lord said, "What have you done? Listen! Your brother's blood cries out to me from the ground. 11 Now you are under a curse and driven from the ground, which opened its mouth to receive your brother's blood from your hand. 12 When you work the ground, it will no longer yield its crops for you. You will be a restless wanderer on the earth."

13 Cain said to the LORD, "My punishment is more than I can bear. 14 Today you are driving me from the land, and I will be hidden from your presence; I will be a restless wanderer on the earth, and whoever finds me will kill me."

15 But the LORD said to him, "Not so; if anyone kills Cain, he will suffer vengeance seven times over." Then the LORD put a mark on Cain so that no one who found him would kill him. 16 So Cain went out from the LORD's presence and lived in the land of Nod, east of Eden.

Introduction

Because of the familiarity of the story, it may hold some new insights for us today if you'll be open to it.

Let me take a couple of side roads and clear up a few things before we get into the real essence of this magnificent story. Side Road 1: What was the mark that Cain received? What mark did God put on Cain? Well, we simply do not know and anyone who claims to know claims to have knowledge that is not in the Bible anywhere. No hint of what it is in this book. But I have heard all kinds of outlandish tales about what that mark was. We simply do not know and there is no way of us knowing.

Second Side Road is a little more interesting. Often when I visit folks, and I used to do this more than I do now, they didn't necessarily appreciate my visit. You know a wife will come to the service and say come by and see us Pastor. And the husband is shaking his head. So I go by and talk with some of these folks. I've just been amazed over the years how quickly many of them will jerk out this side road story. "Well, you know I have trouble with the Bible, Reverend, you know. Where did Cain get his wife?" And I want to say, "I have 7 years of postgraduate work and you're going to stump me with that dumb question, where did Cain get his wife? Come on. Give me a little bit of credit."

Well, let me answer that quickly three ways. There are those who say Adam and Eve had multiple children and they were out multiplying long before Cain and Abel or soon after Cain and Abel. The second option is to take seriously the first creation story in the first chapter of Genesis that says, "God said let us create humankind in our image, after our likeness. And God created them male and female, created He them." [21] So, you got the first creation story with just a whole bunch of people. Third option: The Adam and Eve Story - the word Adam is the Hebrew plural word for 'men.' So, when you take the word Adam, which is Hebrew, God created Adam, men, and put them out there. If you want to literalize the word, bring it over to the English translation, and you have a personal pronoun, Adam. But, that's not what the

---

[21] Genesis 1:26-28

Hebrew means. The Hebrew is the word for plural men. So, you have three options in answering that question.

Let's get to the real essence of the story. Why was Cain rejected? What happened to cause the rejection? We can immediately see the depths of the rejection that drove him to kill his brother. Rejection. It's just hard. Many of you, in fact for most of you, I don't have to say that, because you know it. Because you've tasted it. You felt it. You've been in the presence of it.

In doing the research I went to the web and plugged in 'personal rejection.' Let's see where that takes me. I've done things like that before and it took me to some horrible places. But one of the first places it took me was literary rejection. I was just amazed. Page after page after page. Chat room after chat room. Message board after message board of people dealing with literary rejection. And, I thought as I read a lot of that stuff, I can identify with this. I've got some of that. Don't ever put anything out there if you don't want to be rejected! Somebody's going to reject it. It's going to hurt.

And then I found all kinds of rejection out there in the World Wide Web. People would go all the way back and like I did, create the memory of me and this little 3rd grade red headed girl who I just adored. Every time I could, I would sit beside her. Every time I could I would kind of brush her as I walked by. Never once did I get her to look me in the eye. Not once. And, you know we put down that puppy love kind of stuff. But if you want to read some horrible things, go to the suicide statistics and see how many teenage children killed themselves over the rejection of a puppy love. It can be serious. Deadly serious.

How is it that Cain came to be rejected? He has a marvelous name; he is the firstborn. And in that society, the firstborn received the blessing and received the greater part of the inheritance. In Cain's birth his mother Eve named him "Precious Man from the Lord." So it sounds like he starts off pretty good. He becomes a farmer. His brother Abel becomes a herdsman. They come to the time where they experience a worship service and I suspect they had experienced many. But as adults Able brings what he was instructed to bring - a firstling from his flock without blemish and spots. It is sacrificed on the altar, it's fat portions are burned and offered to the Lord. The smoke that curls up from the offering is indicative of their prayers of worship going to God. Cain on the other hand brings his produce, the products of his blood, sweat and tears. He brings what we would call 'works righteousness' to the offering and presents what he has raised.

"Well, come on, Preacher. Didn't Abel present what he raised?" Yes, he did. But what did they do with it? A sacrifice. Its life was lost. Its life was taken for the payment of their sins. You know you will hear from time to time preachers who make this mistake. They will make that dichotomy of in the Old Testament, people lived by law and in the New Testament, people lived by grace. That is not true. Never happened. No one in the Old Testament ever lived by the law. They were never saved by the law because they couldn't keep the law, just like <u>we</u> can't keep the law.

In the Old Testament they were rightly related to God through the sacrifice of an animal. An innocent animal died in their place. So it was the grace of God, experienced through the sacrifice of that animal dying in their place on their behalf, that rightly related them to God. It is not law in the Old Testament and Grace in the New Testament. It is Grace plus Grace plus Grace. And I remind you that 'Grace is Not a Blue-Eyed Blond." [22] Grace is the Unmerited, Undeserved Joyous Acceptance of God. That's Grace. Abel responds to that Grace and brings his offering as instructed. Cain - works righteousness; 'I want to present what I have done.'

The commentaries go back and forth and argue about exactly why was Cain rejected by God. In Hebrews 11:3, it says that, "By faith Abel offered a better offering than Cain." One could glean from that, that it is a matter of faith, it was a matter of the heart. Cain's heart was not right. Abel's heart was right when they brought their offerings to the Lord.

I John 3:12 says these words. "Cain's actions were evil. Abel's actions were righteous." What does the text say? Listen one more time to verse 6. Then the LORD said to Cain, "Why are you angry? Why is your face downcast? If you do what is right, will you not be accepted?" Cain didn't do anything with his heart. It has everything to do with his action. "Cain if you do what is right will you not be accepted?" What was the

[22] Rollins, Eugene C. Grace Is Not a Blue-Eyed Blond. Bloomington, IN. Author House. 2005

right thing to do? The right thing to do is to be recipients, accepting God's Grace, God's unmerited favor. We cannot work for it. And that, dear friends, is at the core of rejection. Cain wants to be accepted on his terms. Cain wants God's acceptance on his terms, not God's terms. I want to demonstrate that I'm worthy of it. I've worked for it. Here it is. And this ought to please you. But it did not. God rejected it and so will God reject us today. Because God offers to us Grace. Unmerited, Divine forgiveness in the wounds, in the sacrifice of Jesus, the Christ.

Cain said no. And that deep rejection by God created in him such anger that it led him to kill his brother and bury him in the fields that produced the offering that he brought to God. The wounds of rejection can carry us that deeply into evil. And, the church has some judgment to pay in relationship to our rejection of people. The church will be judged for the many little left-handed children that were beat with rulers and told by the church leaders that you are possessed and tied their little left hands behind them. We'll be judged for that. We'll be judged for the rejection of the Red Man whom we called a Savage, and "the only good Savage is a dead one." We'll be judged for that. We'll be judged for the black faces that we looked into and said you are soulless, uneducatable people and unredeemable. The church will be judged for that rejection. And the church will be judged for the rejection that it's spilling out today by rejecting people because of their gender. Do you realize how long we were a country before women had the privilege, the equal acceptance to vote? Thank God I just heard on the news last week women now own the world. Did you know that? I wanted to say, I've known that for 25 years. You've come a long way baby.

I remember a tough fight I had with another congregation in trying to get them to understand that when 1 Timothy 3:12 says, "Let the Deacon, the bishop, be the husband of one wife." What was the predominant issue in the day in which this was written? Was it divorce and remarriage? No. Very little of that was taking place. The woman did not have the right to leave and divorce. She had to tough it out. So there was a little of that taking place. Let the husband who is going to be Bishop or Deacon, be the husband of one wife at a time. What was rampant in that day was polygamy, not divorce and remarriage. The church will be judged for those divorced people who they told you cannot be an elder, you cannot be a deacon, you cannot be a minister because that's what the Bible says. We've got a lot of judgment coming for the rejection that we've handed out.

Cain fell so hard and that's what rejection does to us. It led him to kill his brother out of his anger. Part of that woundedness comes from seeing acceptance. Cain saw the acceptance that Abel, his brother, experienced. We've seen acceptance. We may not be able to define it exactly, just like we're often unable to define love, but you know within your heart whether or not you are loved. You may not be able to define it, describe it, but you know it. You know when it's there and you know when it's not there. Cain looked at the acceptance of Abel and it drove him mad with anger.

Keep in mind with us today the greatest sense of rejection comes from this behavior right here and if you miss everything, don't miss this. When we are so insecure that we are driven compulsorily to live pleasing everybody in the world, we set ourselves up for constant rejection. Constant rejection.

Some years ago I had been rejected by two oral communities defending my written work and supervision in clinical pastoral education. Twice. I went to see a medicine man in Kingstree, South Carolina from Oklahoma, an Oglala Sioux. I got there a little late in his first presentation so I just sat in the back. While he was talking he was whittling. When he finished whittling on this little stick he put it in his pocket. At the close of that presentation he came straight to me working his way through some people and he said, (I'd never met the man before in my life), he said. "People who like you, really, really do like you and the people who don't like you, they really, really don't like you." Immediately those two rejections by the committees came up. He reached in his pocket and pulled out that little whittling stick. It had all kinds of notches on it, and he said, "This is a negative stick. Carry it with you. It will absorb the negativity towards you until you become mature enough to take it yourself." Wow! You think I didn't have that negative stick when I went before the third committee? I had that thing in a little Indian bag around my neck.

We cannot please everybody and when you struggle and strive to do that, you are going to be rejected time after time after time after time.

But the greatest rejection that will pain us the deepest and drive us to insanity is the sense of being rejected by God.

Cain says to God, "My punishment is more than I can bear." Listen to what he says again. "Today you are driving me from the land, and I'll be hidden from your presence; I'll be a restless wanderer on the earth, and whoever finds me will kill me." Let me put that in a way that I think you can remember it better. Cain said my punishment is horrible. I am disconnected. I am disconnected from the land. I'm disconnected from my family of origin. I'm disconnected from those I know the most. I am disconnected. How many times have I heard that from those who feel so sharply the sting of rejection. I don't feel connected; I feel like an outsider. Rejected.

And then Cain says to God another word. I'm hidden from your presence. I am disowned. Disowned. You no longer claim me; I am sent from your presence. Disconnected. Disowned. And then he says to God, I am discomforted, a restless wanderer. Nothing will comfort me no matter how much material world I amass, no matter how popular I become, no matter my riches, my fortune, I am restless. Discomforted. Nothing will fill that hole.

St. Augustine was absolutely right when he wrote hundreds of years ago, "Thou oh Lord, created us for thyself and our hearts will be restless until they rest in Thee." Cain says I'm disconnected from all that I belong to. I'm disowned by my Creator. I'm discomforted; nothing will comfort me. And then finally says, I'll be discovered. I will be found out. The greatest fear of the wounds of rejection is that constant agonizing fear at the core of your soul, "I am going to be discovered. People are going to find out that I'm rejected, disowned, disconnected, discomforted, and now I have been discovered."

Conclusion

Do you have a sense of how hurt, despondent Cain became to the point of killing his brother? The core of rejection is in attempting to please even God with our works righteousness with my church attendance, with my offerings. God says, I want your acceptance of my love-gift in Jesus Christ to you. By his death your transgressions are removed. That's what we come to accept. That is the offering that God our savior wants. And that will place you in Abel's camp and not in Cain's camp of rejection.

Some quick closing statements about rejection.

- Rejection should be our teacher not our undertaker because all of us are going to experience various forms of rejection.
- Rejection is a delay not a defeat on life's journey.
- Rejection is a temporary detour, not a dead end.
- Rejection is just a necessary step on the way to success. It comes to us all.
- Rejection will teach us much more than acceptance if we'll let it, and the greatest barrier to acceptance is the fear of rejection.

Our greatest Glory is not in being never rejected but our greatest glory is in continuing every time that we are.

Let us pray.

Lord, we look at this horrible story in the early beginnings of your Word, shocking though it may be, the killing of one's own flesh and blood. Help us to know this morning how deeply the wounds of rejection can affect us. How insane it can drive us but help us to know oh Lord that the wounds of rejection are wounds that are healable. Healable in the wounds of the song, the writer said, "He is the balm of Gilead that cleanses our sin-sick soul." Help us to come to you accepting your grace, your forgiveness, your sacrifice, your acceptance. May it be so. In Jesus' name. Amen.

May God bless you and keep you healing from all your wounds. God bless you.

WHAT HAPPENS TO US IS NOT THAT IMPORTANT.

IT IS WHAT HAPPENS TO WHAT HAPPENS TO US THAT IS IMPORTANT.

The most skilful physicians are those who, from their youth upwards, have combined with the knowledge of their art the greatest experience of disease;… and should have had all manner of diseases in their own person.

Plato, *Republic*

Chapter 7

SAUL: WOUNDED BY JEALOUSY

Text: 1 Samuel 18:1-9

CIT: *(Central Idea of the text)*
               David gained prominence while Saul grew jealous making
               several attempts to kill him.

Thesis: The wounds of jealousy will carry us into insane behaviors.

Purpose:
   • Major Objective: Supportive
   • Specific Objective: Through the power of the Holy Spirit, I
     hope to lead each of us out of our insecurity which produces
     jealousy.

Introduction

Outline:
   I.   Wounds of Jealousy Begin With Insecurity - vs. 6-8
   II.   Wounds of Jealousy Will Consume Us - v. 10
   III. Wounds of Jealousy Will Carry Us Into Insane Behaviors -
         vs.18:10-11; 18:17-30; 19:1; 19:9-10; 19:11-24

Conclusion:

*"...internal insecurity
produces a partner.
And, that partner is fear."*

"Jealousy is a cancer,
an internal cancer,
and its cause is
our own insecurity."

The Word of the Lord

1 Samuel 18:1-9

1 After David had finished talking with Saul, Jonathan became one in spirit with David, and he loved him as himself. 2 From that day Saul kept David with him and did not let him return to his father's house. 3 And Jonathan took off the robe he was wearing and gave it to David, along with his tunic, and even his sword, his bow and his belt.

5 Whatever Saul sent him to do, David did it so successfully that Saul gave him a high rank in the army. This pleased all the people, and Saul's officers as well.

6 When the men were returning home after David had killed the Philistine, the women came out from all the towns of Israel to meet King Saul with singing and dancing, with joyful songs and with tambourines and lutes. 7 As they danced, they sang:

"Saul has slain his thousands,

and David his tens of thousands."

8 Saul was very angry; this refrain galled him. "They have credited David with tens of thousands," he thought, "but me with only thousands. What more can he get but the kingdom?"

9 And from that time on Saul kept a jealous eye on David.

Introduction

Wounded by jealousy. The Bible has nothing pleasant, complimentary at all to say about jealousy.

Psalm 79:5, "Jealousy burns like fire."

Proverbs 6:4, "Jealousy creates fury."

Song of Solomon 8:6, "Jealousy is as unyielding as the grave."

The Bible has nothing good to say about jealousy. Shakespeare had nothing good to say about jealousy. He wrote, "The venom clamors of a jealous woman poison more deadly than a mad dog's tooth." Wow!

Roger Dangerfield said, "My wife's jealousy is getting ridiculous. Last week she was looking in my calendar and asked me who May was."

Jeff Foxworthy said, "I've never been jealous. I was not even jealous when my father graduated from the 5th grade a year before I did."

In the poem My Jealousy is My Madness the poet Sri Chinmoy put it like this:

"Jealousy, before you entered my life, I was the world's richest prince.
Now that you are in me and I am for you I have become a poor street beggar.
You are my constant nightmare-mind; you are my constant love-absence-heart.
Shortest is the distance from jealousy to hell. Jealousy, you are your own
ultimate self-destructive-indulgence."

Paris Hilton has a very popular song entitled Jealousy. The chorus goes like this:

"Jealousy, Jealousy, Jealousy
Is such an evil thing
To watch someone have
Jealousy, Jealousy, Jealousy
Nobody wins when you're full of envy."

Saul, the scriptures tell us, in the 9th chapter of 1 Samuel, was selected by God to be Israel's first king. And the scriptures tell us he was above all men impressively handsome. He was head and shoulders taller than anyone in his town. Samuel the prophet came, called forth Saul and Samuel anointed him as God's chosen one to be king of Israel.

And then, along comes this kid, this shepherd kid, David, who with a slingshot slays the giant Goliath who had intimidated all of Israel for months. Immediately, the people rallied around him. King Saul admitted him to his household to play his harp for his depression. That was the first experience of music therapy that is widely used in mental hospitals and some psychiatric hospitals today. It works. And, then realizing the boy's military mind and strength, King Saul would send him out to fight the enemies around. After one of those engagements David and Saul were coming back into the city and the people were shouting, "Saul has killed his thousands and David his ten thousands." From that moment on the scriptures tell us that Saul kept a jealous eye on David.

What we will see is that jealousy absolutely consumes the man, this impressive, handsome, anointed one, son of God. It is just heartbreaking to see how the cancer, the malignancy of jealously takes hold of him and brings him to the depths of suicide. That's what jealousy will do. I couldn't find a statistic so I can only speak out of my own clinical experience. I have been seeing couples for 55 years. In my clinical experience jealousy causes more divorce than infidelity. In fact, I can work a couple through infidelities easier, quicker than I can when one of the spouses is eaten up with jealousy. Because you see, we do exactly what Saul did. It was not Saul's issue. It was David's issue. It was projected outside of Saul.

Look at this man. He is so impressive, the people are running around saying that he has killed tens of thousands. Saul has just killed a thousand. No indication whatsoever that Saul takes an internal look. None at all. Jealousy begins with internal insecurity. We don't want to believe that. "If he/she wouldn't do this or that I wouldn't be jealous." I have spouses coming to me wanting me to do a personality transplant on the extroverted spouse that they have. "Everywhere she goes, she just flirts with everybody." I say, "She's just being who she is. She's an extrovert! That's not her issue; that's your issue."

Is there scripture for that, preacher? Yes, there is. Did you hear what Saul said in verse 9? "What more can he get but the kingdom?" That internal insecurity produces a partner. And, that partner is fear. And, Saul is insecure about his ability to hold the kingdom and he is fearful that David is going to become so popular, that he will rise above him and usurp his kingship. Retranslated today - we are so insecure we become fearful that our spouse, lover, significant other is going to find someone just a little more charming than we are, just a little more handsome than we are, just a little more beautiful than we are with just a little more money and pizzazz than we have. We live out that fear in the attempt to control. "I'll just lock her down. I'll get up every morning before she does and write down the mileage on the car." In fact we have gotten so technologically advanced, "I'll put me one of those tracker gizmos on it and it'll tell me on my computer 24/7 where she is."

It is always externalized. If I can structure it, make it secure, externally out here, I won't be jealous. If I can control him/her to the point of where I know where he/she is any time of the day, any time of the week, I'll feel okay." Not so. Because we are trying to answer an internal question with an external answer and it never works. The other partner trying to feed that is like taking a fire extinguisher filled with pure oxygen and blowing it on fire.

Finally, the minister comes to me and he said, "This is the last straw."

"Tell me about it."

He said, "In my town there are three major hospitals. My wife has demanded I visit the hospitals Monday, Wednesday and Friday. She has demanded that I call her on Monday, tell her how many parishioners I have in the hospital and where they are. She has traveled those three hospitals. She has given me an allotted amount of time, five minutes per visit per parishioner." And, he said, "I can't take it anymore. This is the last straw."

I asked him what he had been doing all these years? He said, "Just what I do now. I give her the list every Monday morning. I call her as soon as I get back to the church. If I'm not on time, she reprimands and wants to know where I have been."

That only fuels the fire. How many times do I hear, "I am so worried, I want to protect her. I don't really want to control her. I just want to know where she is. I'm not really insecure. I just want to know what she's doing."

Jealousy is a cancer. An internal cancer and its cause is our own insecurity. As long as we attempt to control, deal with the other person - the object of our jealousy - it will never ever clear up. It will never ever change until the jealous one starts asking, "Why am I this way? What is it in me that is creating this awesome fear?"

It will consume you, as it consumed Saul. He brings David in to play his harp and while he's playing, he reaches behind him, on two different occasions, and tries to spear him to the wall. David dodges the spear.

Saul says, "I'm going to kill him," and he puts him in command of every battle that comes up. David is to be there in front with his men against the enemy. Saul is consumed. It's all he can think about. He lies awake at night thinking, "He's going to get my kingdom. I can not keep my kingdom."

The third point I want to make is that if something is not done about this wound of jealousy, which is insecurity that produces fear, it will drive us to absolute insane behavior. The jealous one can't see it. But anyone else can look at that behavior and just shake their head. What you're doing, what you are thinking is absolutely insane.

There are two clear examples here. Saul is pursuing David. He is camped at night. He is in a cave at night, asleep with his men around him. David slips in the cave in the dead of night and takes his knife and cuts off the bottom of King Saul's robe. And, then in the dawn he cries from the other side of the creek, "Oh, King. You who God anointed, you who I serve, look at the bottom of your robe." He holds up the piece of robe that he cut from the king's robe. He says, "This could have been your head." No one knew it. No one stopped me. This piece of cloth could have been your head. I do not want to harm you. I do not want your palace. I do not want your kingdom. I wish you no harm.

Did it help? Yep, for 5 minutes! King Saul said, "Oh my son. Bless you. I'm sorry. You are the good one and I'm the bad one. Please come back to the palace." David didn't fall off the turnip truck last week. He didn't go back. Saul continued to pursue. Consumed. He was consumed with jealousy to kill the object of his fear. [23]

Spouses don't want to kill their spouses - well, some do. It happens in South Carolina. South Carolina happens to be one of the leading states in spousal deaths. I hope you know that. They just want to control. Saul can't control him. He can't control the people's joyous response.

So, on the second occasion, David finds Saul camped in a cave asleep. He slips in. Saul's spear is sticking in the ground beside his head and his bottle of water is on the other side of his head. David takes his spear and his jug of water, goes across the valley and waits until daylight. He says to the king, "The men around you, you ought to put to death. If you want to put somebody to death, you ought to those around you

---

[23] Sanford, John A. King Saul, the Tragic Hero. New York: Paulist Press 1985

who did not and could not protect you. Look, your spear and your water jug. Once again, I could have lifted your head."

Does this change the man? No. Is his wound of jealousy healed? No. When we are wounded, we will become wounded healers or we will become wounded wounders. And, Saul, out of his woundedness, becomes a wounded wounder. Driven, consumed by the insane pursuit. Jealousy will do that to you. If you are here this morning and that is one of your unhealed wounds, I pray to God that maybe for the first time in your life that you will say, "It has nothing at all to do with my boss, with my job, with my spouse or anyone else. It has everything to do with me."

Conclusion

I've struggled with insecurity all my life. I remember so vividly being in the Will Rogers museum in Ft. Worth, Texas. He was from Oklahoma but the museum was in Fort Worth. There on the wall was a picture of Will Rogers and right under it was this statement: "All men are ignorant about something." I stood there, read that and wept. I am ignorant about something. You are ignorant about something. I know about stuff you don't know. You know stuff I don't know. We are all ignorant about something. It was this 'ah-ha' moment, Gestalt moment in my life. I believe to one degree or another all of us are wounded by jealousy. Whether or not it will consume us depends on us and depends on what degree we will do self-reflection, self-insight in turning that over to our divine Healer, Jesus the Christ, who is said of him in Psalm 147, verse 3, "He heals the brokenhearted and binds up their wounds." Unlike Saul who could have gone back in his thought processes and said, "I am God's anointed one. God anointed me. This kingdom is mine until God chooses to take it away. Until that time I will be faithful because I am God's elect."

He couldn't do that. He wouldn't do that. And, it's just the same with us. We will not go deep within and say to ourselves, "I am a child of God, created as a spirit of my spirit God. In my spiritual walk, and in my earthly walk, God will heal the wounds that come to me. They will be healed!" The wonderful Gospel story says Jesus bore our stripes. "By his stripes we are healed." Does not the scripture tell us, "God is not a god of fear but of love and of a sound mind?" (2 Timothy 1:7) Do not allow the wound of jealousy to destroy your marriage, your relationship, your job, your life. There is no need for you to be that insecure and fearful. God loves you and is with you. God desires to heal you.

Let us pray.

Oh Lord, thank you for this tragic story. A story of a life, selected, called and anointed by you that went awry. But then oh God, we all go awry. We are all wounded. Help us to confess our woundedness. Help us to seek healing in You who binds up our wounds and heals the brokenhearted, that we might make healing contributions to our communities, marriages, families, and society. God help us not to perpetuate our woundedness onto others. May it be so. In Jesus' name. Amen.

May God bless you and keep you healing from all your wounds. God bless you.

WHAT HAPPENS TO US IS NOT THAT IMPORTANT.

IT IS WHAT HAPPENS TO WHAT HAPPENS TO US THAT IS IMPORTANT.

Stephen Colbert was born on May 13, 1964 in Washington, DC but was raised on James Island, South Carolina. He was the youngest of eleven children. He was wounded on September 11, 1974 with the death of his father and his two closet brothers when they were killed in an Eastern Airlines crash in Charlotte, North Carolina. He has also been wounded having to deal with depression and anxiety. Yet, he is an actor, writer, producer and comedian healing many through his humor. He is a devout Roman Catholic and an ordained minister with the Universal Life Church Monastery.

CHAPTER 8

SAMSON: WOUNDED BY LOVE

Text: Judges 16:15-30

CIT: *(Central Idea of the text)*
            Sampson was mortally wounded by his love for Delilah.

Thesis: The Wounds of Love Can Be Mortal.

Purpose:
- Major Objective: Supportive
- Specific Objective: Through the power of the Holy Spirit, I hope to lead each of us in working through our wounds of love.

Introduction

Outline:
    I.   Wounding Love Is Often Unequal - vs. 16:4 & 15
    II.   Wounding Love is Often Repeated - vs. 14:1-20
    III.   Wounding Love Can Be Lethal – vs. 16:25-30

Conclusion:

*"Unequal love
often betrays."*

The Word of the Lord

Judges 16:15-30

15 Then she said to him, "How can you say, 'I love you,' when you won't confide in me? This is the third time you have made a fool of me and haven't told me the secret of your great strength."

16 With such nagging she prodded him day after day until he was tired to death.

17 So he told her everything. "No razor has ever been used on my head," he said, "because I have been a Nazirite set apart to God since birth. If my head were shaved, my strength would leave me, and I would become as weak as any other man."

18 When Delilah saw that he had told her everything, she sent word to the rulers of the Philistines, "Come back once more; he has told me everything." So the rulers of the Philistines returned with the silver in their hands. 19 Having put him to sleep on her lap, she called a man to shave off the seven braids of his hair, and so began to subdue him. And his strength left him.

20 Then she called, "Samson, the Philistines are upon you!" He awoke from his sleep and thought, "I'll go out as before and shake myself free." But he did not know that the LORD had left him.

21. Then the Philistines seized him, gouged out his eyes and took him down to Gaza. Binding him with bronze shackles, they set him to grinding in the prison. 22 But the hair on his head began to grow again after it had been shaved.

23 Now the rulers of the Philistines assembled to offer a great sacrifice to Dagon their god and to celebrate, saying, "Our god has delivered Samson, our enemy, into our hands."

24 When the people saw him, they praised their god, saying, "Our god has delivered our enemy into our hands, the one who laid waste our land and multiplied our slain."

25 While they were in high spirits, they shouted, "Bring out Samson to entertain us." So they called Samson out of the prison, and he performed for them. When they stood him among the pillars, 26 Samson said to the servant who held his hand, "Put me where I can feel the pillars that support the temple, so that I may lean against them.

27 Now the temple was crowded with men and women; all the rulers of the Philistines were there, and on the roof were about three thousand men and women watching Samson perform. 28 Then Samson prayed to the LORD, "O Sovereign LORD, remember me. O God, please strengthen me just once more, and let me with one blow get revenge on the Philistines for my two eyes." 29 Then Samson reached toward the two central pillars on which the temple stood. Bracing himself against them, his right hand on the one and his left hand on the other, 30 Samson said, "Let me die with the Philistines!" Then he pushed with all his might, and down came the temple on the rulers and all the people in it. Thus he killed many more when he died than when he lived.

Introduction

(Gene singing before the scripture is read) "Far across the deep blue waters lived an Old German's daughter by the banks of the old River Rhyne. Where I loved her and left her but I can't forget her, she is my pretty Fraulein." [24]

That's for all you old people! We're the only ones who can remember that one.

Our world is filled with songs of wounded love. It's filled with wounded lovers. All of us here this morning have been wounded by love to some degree, in some fashion, and in some way.

Alfred Lord Tennyson said, "Tis better to have loved and lost than never to have loved at all." Many would not agree with poet Tennyson. Many others have said, "Love begins with a smile, grows with a kiss, and ends with a teardrop."

Socrates said, "The hottest love has the coldest end."

January 12, 2010 Psychology Today magazine had an article entitled, "Loves Walking Wounded." They gave many accounts of how love had wounded individuals. In their research they said that they see three responses often in this wounding. One is, after being wounded by love, one will be hyper-vigilant about getting involved in this kind of emotional bonding again. So they have their tentacles out and just very, very sensitive, hypersensitive, to that kind of emotion.

---

[24] Fraulein was written by Lawton Williams and sung often by Willie Nelson

A second group they said is the group that just hardens themselves and that's usually the group that does the deepest wounding of others out of their grief.

The third category they said just simply opt out and are not going to get involved in anything like that again. In Freud's words, Freud would say they would compensate in some other area. Work harder, recreate harder, do something to compensate for this need, this vacuum within their lives.

Psychology Today went on to say that there were three very important components to keep one in a healthy love, a love that would not be wounded. That was passion, intimacy, and commitment. They went on to say that any two of those without the third is like a three-legged stool that will not stand. Passion. Intimacy. Commitment. [25]

There is a Spanish proverb that says, "Where there is love there is pain." I remember years ago working with a client wounded by love. I asked her to define love for me and she said, and I quote, "It's lying down on the interstate and letting an 18-wheeler run over you." Oh wow! I had some work to do.

Sam Keen in his book "To Love and Be Loved," made this statement: "In the depths of our being, in body, soul, and mind, we know intuitively that we are created to love and to be loved. Fulfilling this imperative, responding to this vocation, is the central meaning of life." I believe Keen's to be a true statement. I believe our Lord said the same thing in many different ways. That the most important goal, search, the deepest meaning is that of loving, giving yourself in it, and being loved in return. I believe it to be the most powerful emotion in the world today.

In his classic work "The Art of Loving," Erich Fromm made this statement, "In spite of the deep-seated craving for love almost everything else is considered to be more important than love. Success, privilege, money, power - almost all our energy is used for learning how to achieve these aims and almost no one learns The Art of Loving." I thought, "Wow! What a powerful statement!" It is one of our deepest yearnings. It is the central meaning of our lives but we then give out all

[25] Psychology Today (Jan. 12, 2010) written by John R. Buri, Phd.

of our energy to earning money, power, success, popularity, recognition. No wonder we're in trouble.

This little fascinating story of Samson and these two women, I believe, give us some insight, some principles that will help us to avoid loves deep wounding. First of all, I'm seeing this story not just in our texts but in the earlier chapters of Judges, that when love is unequal you can depend upon the wounding; in other words, when one person loves the other person and the other person does not love in return.

Sheldon Kopp, in his eschatological laundry list, number 14 says, "You can't make anyone love you."[26] And you can't. I don't care how hard you try. I don't care how hard you gift-give them, how hard you pursue them, you can't make someone love you. And when Love is unequal you're in for a wounding.

Samson goes down to Gaza and he meets this woman. He comes back and he tells his mom and daddy, (listen to this classical statement) in Chapter 14 verse 3, "She is the right one for me." How many times have I heard that? Mom and Daddy say to him, "Can't you find a wife among the Israelites? Must you go down there?" He said, "She's the right one for me. Let's go get her."

Well, on the way down there they are attacked by a lion and Samson kills it with his bare hands. They go on and I guess exchange a dowry and the wedding feast is set up. A 7-day feast. And on the way back down there for the marriage and the feast, he comes upon the carcass of this lion that he killed sometime back. In the carcass there is a hive of honey bees. So, he gets some honey, eats it, gives it to his parents and he makes up this little poem. He says in this little poem, "Out of the eater comes something to eat. Out of the strong, something sweet." (Judges 14:14)

So he goes on down to Gaza, gets ready for the feast. He says to some of those that his future wife has invited, "Let me tell you a riddle and if you guess the riddle I'll give you 30 changes of clothes. If you don't guess the riddle in the 7 day feast, you give me 30 changes of clothes." They said okay, give us the riddle. So Samson gave them the riddle.

---

[26] Kopp, Sheldon B. If You Meet the Buddha on the Road, Kill Him. New York: Bantam Boos 1972, p. 223

Before the close of the seventh day, they could not guess the riddle. They convinced Samson's wife to share the riddle. She didn't know it but she seduced Samson into telling her the riddle. Then, she shared it with her own ethnic tribe. Samson had to come up with 30 changes of clothes. He did what Samson usually did. He went to another town, killed thirty other Philistines and took their clothes off and brought them back. He felt so betrayed that he went back to Israel leaving his first wife.

No indication in that story anywhere, and by the way this woman is unnamed, no indication that she loved him. He said that she said to him, if you really love me you'll tell me this riddle. Well he did and then she betrayed him. Unequal love often betrays. And, to me it is heart rendering. At times it's amusing to see into the world of clients how determined one can become to make the other person love them quote, "As much as I love you." It will not happen. If you're in that situation where you feel like you love this person and they don't love you like you love them, exit my friend. Find the little red sign somewhere that says Exit and take it because it's not going to grow. It's not going to change. You are in for a wounding.

It's astonishing to me that on these two occasions, Samson's first wife and then his relationship with Delilah, are exactly the same. Unequal. No indication that either one of these women loved him. And I repeat, when you're in that situation you cannot make it happen. As Kopp says, "You can't make someone love you."

Samson goes back down after a period of time and meets Delilah. He falls in love with her and, again, it is unequal love. In his relationship with her, it is the second principle in this text that I want to lift out for you and it is so very, very clear. First, do not get involved in an unequal relationship. They will wound you. Secondly, be careful of repeating the same mistake you made last time. I see that again and again and again. We keep marrying the same kind of person time after time.

A person said to me last week, this is my fourth one. I'm gonna keep doing it till I get it right! And I wanted to say, well if you wouldn't keep hooking up with the same kind of person, maybe you wouldn't repeat it.

But here is Samson hooked up with Delilah and she is offered a large sum of money by her ethnic tribe. These are Arabs, by the way.

She says to Samson, tell me the source of your great strength. If you really love me you will keep nothing from me. You'll be totally honest with me so tell me the source of your mighty power.

Samson says to her, if I am tied with 7 green thongs then my strength will be gone. I'll be as weak as any other man. So she says that to her clan, they go get seven green thongs and she seduces him. He's asleep. She ties him up and then yells, "The Philistines are here." Samson jumps up, breaks them, whips them all, sends them running. She is upset and as that text says, keeps pressuring him. Nagging, I think, is the word they use. He says to her the second time, if I am tied with new ropes, ropes that have never been used before, I will lose my strength. She seduces him. He's asleep in her lap. She tied him up with 7 virgin ropes and hollers, "The Philistines are here!" He jumps up, breaks the ropes like they were strings, whips them and sends them running. She is so upset. Nothing is said about his upsetness. Duh!

What's it going to take? You keep repeating this time and time again. What is it going to take, Samson? Finally, this is the word she puts on him, "If you really love me, how can you say you love me and you will not confide the truth with me?" He says, okay maybe I can trust her this time. It is like hold the football for me one more time. Don't you just love that in the comic strip? Maybe this time Lucy won't pick it up. She's changed. My love for her has changed her. My concern for her has changed her. She won't pick it up this time. She always picks it up.

Samson says to her, if you cut these seven locks of my hair, I'll lose my strength. She seduces him. He sleeps on her lap. She shaves the seven locks of hair. Same story. Same story. Three times! Same story. Finally he gives in and he says to her, "I'm a Nazarene. If my hair is cut, there lies my strength." He goes to sleep the final time and she cuts his hair. She yells, "The Philistines are here!" He jumps up and they whip him like a yard dog. His strength is gone. He is a beaten, wounded man. Wounded by his love of a woman who did not love him.

The first thing they do is gorge his eyes out. Here's a picture of this mighty man of God, blind leading a grinding stone as the mules and the oxen used to do. Say what you will about what followed but you cannot get away from the fact that Samson was so wounded by his betrayal, so physically blind, and so mentally depressed, he killed himself. Yes, he took some of the enemy with him but he killed himself. Pure and simple.

One point. Three million people in the United States every year out of their love-wounds, wound others. There are 1.3 million people involved in domestic violence every year in this country. It cost us $4.1 billion just for the medical care of people hurt in domestic relationships by wounded love. In South Carolina there are 35,000 to 40,000 cases every year. This is just the reported violence in South Carolina. 35,000 to 45,000 every year! 28% of all the deaths in South Carolina are domestic-related.[27] Wounded by love and we become wounded wounders. Not seeking to have the love healed; not having it healed. We embrace it and we become it, i.e., wounded wounders.

In 1967 I was pastoring a little Mission Church in Spartanburg County and attending Wofford College. A young attractive mother of two came to my office, spent an hour and a half, unraveling a tale of love's wounding. She went home, locked herself in her bedroom, shot herself in the head. I was the last person she ever talked to. Wounded love can be lethal. The wounds of love are not to be taken lightly. As recent as this year sitting across from me, he looks at his estranged wife and he looks at me, and he looks back at her and he says, "I cannot live without you." Before the next session that next week, he had committed suicide. Wounded love is not to be taken lightly. Few wounds in our lives can wound us as deeply as love gone awry, i.e., when it is unequal and when we keep repeating the same scenario.

Conclusion

But there is healing. For you see the wounded love that I'm talking about is the same kind of love wound that carried Jesus to the cross. That verse that you learned at your mama's knee, "For God so loved the world that he gave." God gave God's self in Jesus the Christ. Ultimately he gave himself on Calvary's tree. And in that beautiful verse in Romans 5:8, God demonstrates his love to us. "While we were yet sinners Christ died for us." That is our hope ladies and gentlemen. That in our

---

[27] National Coalition Against Domestic Violence: Domestic Violence Facts: South Carolina (2010)

wounding, we go to Him who took our Stripes upon himself. Wounded on our behalf. And the wounds of the cross were love-wounds. God loved us so much that he was willing to allow Jesus the Christ to come, have his love rejected to such an extent that it carried him to Calvary's tree. And by his stripes we are healed. Carry your love-wounds to the cross for Christ's healing. Rather than becoming hyper-vigilant or hardened, carry your love disappointment to the healing of Christ who died for you.

Let us pray.

Oh Lord, for this tragic love story of love gone awry, we give you thanks and praise for the recording of it. Help us to learn from the mistakes of Samson's life. Help us to know how deeply you love us. And help us to know that your love of us will ultimately never wound us but will ultimately heal us if we will bring our wounds, whatever they may be, even the deep disappointing love wounds, you will heal us. And bring us to the point of being recipients of your love to where we can love and be loved by each other once again. May it be so in each of our lives here today. In Jesus' name. Amen.

May God bless you and keep you healing and loving. God bless you.

WHAT HAPPENS TO US IS NOT THAT IMPORTANT.

**IT IS WHAT HAPPENS TO WHAT HAPPENS
TO US THAT IS IMPORTANT**.

"Our brilliance, our juiciness, our spiciness, is all mixed up with our craziness and our confusion, and therefore it doesn't do any good to try to get rid of our so-called negative aspects, because in that process we also get rid of our basic wonderfulness. Our pain and suffering is part of our wonderfulness; our wounds are part of our wonderfulness. We can probably even say that without our pain and suffering, without our wounds, we would have no wonderfulness."

Pema Chodron

CHAPTER 9

DAVID: WOUNDED BY INFIDELITY

Text: 2 Samuel 11:1-27

CIT: *(Central Idea of the text)*
           King David and Bathsheba were wounded by infidelity.

Thesis: The wounds of infidelity can lead a person into insane behaviors.

Purpose:
- Major Objective: Ethical/Actional
- Specific Objective: Through the power of the Holy Spirit, I hope to lead us in healing from the wounds of infidelity.

Introduction

Outline:
   I.   David Committed to Being at the Wrong Place at the Wrong Time – v. 1
  II.   David Committed Emotional Infidelity – vs. 2-3
 III. David Committed Physical Infidelity – v. 4
 IV. David Committed Deception with Uriah – vs. 6-13
  V.   David Committed the Murder of Uriah – vs.14-25
 VI. David Committed Marriage to Bathsheba – v. 27
VII. David Committed a Sin Against God – v. 27

Conclusion:

"Infidelity almost always begins with what therapists call 'Emotional Adultery.' A very high percentage of infidelity takes place at work and it always begins with 'Emotional Adultery.'"

The Word of the Lord

2 Samuel 11:1-27

1 In the spring, at the time when kings go off to war, David sent Joab out with the king's men and the whole Israelite army. They destroyed the Ammonites and besieged Rabbah. But David remained in Jerusalem.

2 One evening David got up from his bed and walked around on the roof of the palace. From the roof he saw a woman bathing. The woman was very beautiful, 3 and David sent someone to find out about her. The man said, "Isn't this Bathsheba, the daughter of Eliam and the wife of Uriah the Hittite?" 4 Then David sent messengers to get her. She came to him, and he slept with her. (She had purified herself from her uncleanness.) Then she went back home. 5 The woman conceived and sent word to David, saying, "I am pregnant."

6 So David sent this word to Joab: "Send me Uriah the Hittite." And Joab sent him to David. When Uriah came to him, David asked him how Joab was, how the soldiers were and how the war was going. 8 Then David said to Uriah, "Go down to your house and wash your feet." So Uriah left the palace, and a gift from the king was sent after him. 9 But Uriah slept at the entrance to the palace with all his master's servants and did not go to his house.

10 When David was told, "Uriah did not go home," he asked him, "Haven't you just come home from a distance? Why didn't you go home?"

11 Uriah said to David, "The ark and Israel and Judah are staying in tents, and my master Joab and my lord's men are camped in the open fields. How could I go to my house to eat and drink and lie with my wife? As surely as you live, I will not do such a thing!"

12 Then David said to him, "Stay here one more day, and tomorrow I will send you back." So Uriah remained in Jerusalem that day and the next. 13 At David's invitation, he ate and drank with him and David made him drunk. But in the evening Uriah went out to sleep on his mat among his master's servants; he did not go home.

14 In the morning David wrote a letter to Joab and sent it with

Uriah. 15 In it he wrote, "Put Uriah in the front line where the fighting is fiercest. Then withdraw from him so he will be struck down and die."

16 So while Joab had the city under siege, he put Uriah at a place where he knew the strongest defenders were. 17 When the men of the city came out and fought against Joab, some of the men in David's army fell; moreover, Uriah the Hittite was dead.

18 Joab sent David a full account of the battle. He instructed the messenger: "When you have finished giving the king this account of the battle, the king's anger may flare up, and he may ask you, 'Why did you get so close to the city to fight: Didn't you know they would shoot arrows from the wall? Who killed Abimelech son of Jerub-Besheth? Didn't a woman throw an upper millstone on him from the wall, so that he died in Thebez? Why did you get so close to the wall?' If he asks you this, then say to him. 'Also, your servant Uriah the Hittite is dead.'"

22 The messenger set out, and when he arrived he told David everything Joab had sent him to say. 23 The messenger said to David, "The men overpowered us and came out against us in the open, but we drove them back to the entrance to the city gate. 24 Then the archers shot arrows at your servants from the wall, and some of the king's men died. Moreover, your servant Uriah the Hittite is dead."

25 David told the messenger, "Say this to Joab: 'Don't let this upset you; the sword devours one as well as another. Press the attack against the city and destroy it.' Say this to encourage Joab."

26 When Uriah's wife heard that her husband was dead, she mourned for him. 27 After the time of mourning was over, David had her brought to his house, and she became his wife and bore him a son. But the thing David had done displeased the Lord.

Introduction

In my clinical practice infidelity is the second most presenting issue. It is a "Big" issue in my work. It is a "Big" issue in the Bible. It is number six on the Bible's "Big Ten List." "Thou shalt not commit adultery." (Ex. 20:14) It comes just after "Thou shalt not commit murder." It is a "Big" deal. The term "adultery" is used 31 times in the Old Testament and

23 times in the New Testament for a total of 54 times. It is also a "Big" deal in our culture today.

In my clinical experience 40 to 60 percent of married couples have been wounded by infidelity. That is in line with the national research. In the U.S. in 2019 there were 782,038 divorces and that was with four states not reporting at all. Fifty percent of all marriages end in divorce with 60 percent of marriages ending that were begun with persons between the ages of 20-25. Twenty to forty percent of married couples have had an extramarital affair sometime during their marriage. There was a time in our history when it was almost always the male spouse but that is no longer true today. I will have as many female spouses as male spouses in today's world.

This tragic story of the life of King David can teach us much about the wounds of infidelity. First of all David was at the wrong place at the wrong time. The text tells us that it was the time of year when "kings went off to war with their army" but King David remained in Jerusalem at the palace. He was not where he should have been.

A husband, father of two, comes into see me all eaten up with guilt. He loves his wife and family but while he was in New York at a work conference he had a lapse of good judgment. After a meeting one night he goes to a night club, has a few drinks, belly rubs on the dance floor with one of the women and it's off to the races. He was at the wrong place at the wrong time. He should have been in his hotel room face-timing his wife and children. Like David he was at the wrong place at the wrong time.

She said to me: "I can't believe it happened." She left her work cubicle every morning at 10 o'clock. Went down to the floor level where there was a Starbucks, got a cup of latte and went back upstairs and worked. They greeted each other first with their eyes, then their voice and then a suggestion that they sit and enjoy their coffee and conversation. "We never meant for anything like that to happen. We both love our spouses and families." She was at the wrong place at the wrong time and it can begin as simple as that.

One evening David was walking around on the flat roof of the palace and saw this beautiful woman bathing. David lusted after her but it could have ended right there. Jesus said, "...I tell you that anyone who looks at a woman lustfully has already committed adultery with her in his heart." (Matthew 5:28). But trust me your wife will not agree with Jesus' statement. It is not as bad to think about it as it is to do it. This is her position – trust me! Jesus was saying that it was a matter of the heart and we should deal with it on a heart level.

Jimmy Carter was wrong when he said on national TV that he was an "adulterer" because he had lusted. Looking and thinking will not get you into the trouble that acting will get you into. But it is where acting begins.

David had Bathsheba checked out and later communicated with her. Infidelity almost always begins with what therapists call "emotional adultery." A very high percentage of infidelity takes place at work and it always begins with "emotional adultery."

He said to me, "I sent her a text that was just a little off color and she thought it was cute." This play progresses to sharing things with your "work wife" that you do not share with your wife. This is explained by saying, "we are just friends." How many times have I heard that?

David's emotional infidelity progresses to physical infidelity. He sent for her and no one says "no" to the king even if she wanted to. Her husband was off at war and she was lonely missing the sight, the smells, the touch of a man. Is that why she was bathing somewhat publicly? It does little good to blame her or David. Seek not to blame but to understand. David had more wives than he could count and she had a husband although away serving his country. Why? Emotional infidelity almost always becomes physical unless one or both realize that they are emotionally involved and contract with themselves or with each other not to act upon their feelings. By this time the old saying, "You don't get your sex and salary at the same place" is thrown out the window. The Biblical saying, "Bread eaten in secret is sweet" has taken over. (Proverbs 9:17) No marriage can compete with the secretive, sneaky, stealthy, shrouded clandestine affair of the heart.

The text reads like David had this one night with Bathsheba but human nature tells me that it was an ongoing affair until she became pregnant. But what is hidden in darkness will come to light, it almost always does. David had been found out and so begins his deception. He brings Uriah home from the war expecting him to have sex with his wife while he is at home. But Uriah is such a man of honor he will not eat at home and sleep with his wife while his fellow soldiers are sleeping in the fields. He sleeps on the ground at the gates of the palace. Therefore, David cannot blame Bathsheba's being pregnant on her husband. I have heard all kinds of deception.

A wife was looking in her husband's truck for a receipt for something when she found a gross of condoms. When she confronted him he said, "I put them on the tale pipe of my truck and watch them burst." In meeting with me, he kept to his story. I can't make this stuff up.

A mother told her teenage son who saw her in another town with a man other than his father, "Honey that was not me. You were simply mistaken."

A wife will find a text and he says, "We are only friends. She is having marital problems and needs someone to talk to. We are just friends." How many, many time have I heard this song and dance.

At this stage David is asking himself, "How in the world did I get into this mess?" And he really can't explain how it all unfolded. If the husband can't explain how and why it happened the wife can't believe it won't happen again. I always say to the offending spouse, "You are 100% responsible for the infidelity. There are always many other choices you could have made but you made this choice." And I always say to the offended spouse, "This was not your fault. You are not innocent but this decision was not yours."

David is caught between a rock and a hard place. So, he has Uriah placed at the front of the battle where he is surely to be killed and he is. Therefore, David murdered Uriah. You would be amazed at the number of times this type of action is taken. South Carolina is the third leading state in spousal deaths. It is a leading state in domestic violence. When one is caught up in this type web of deception one is capable of anything. In this situation one's lawyer will tell the client, "Lie, lie, lie. Do not tell the truth. You will be sued for adultery." I am in the middle of this web trying to bring light to darkness, truth to falsehood and healing to woundness.

Out of his guilt David marries Bathsheba. The highest percentage of people do not marry the people they had the affair with, but those who do have a 72% divorce rate. It is the highest divorce rate within any subset of marriages. The second highest rate is with persons who were pregnant when they were married. David and Bathsheba meet both of these. They would not have divorced because kings put their wives to death. They didn't divorce them and wives could not divorce their "King husband." But their marriage was greatly dysfunctional and very unhealthy. Is it that people who commit infidelity are bad people? Absolutely not! "David was a man after God's own Heart." God called David a friend. Good people, loving spouses are wounded in this way. There is no easy answer as to why it happens. It is complicated.

In the next chapter, 2 Samuel 12, David is confronted by the prophet Nathan anad he confesses his sin. Yes, sin! We don't call it that in today's world. It is a mistake, a lapse of good judgment. Whatever happened to the word "sin?" It is not politically correct to use that word anymore. But it is. A good word that is right on target. It means to "miss the mark." When one is unfaithful sexually to one's spouse one has missed the mark of a committed marriage. Missing that mark will cause a truthful person to become a liar. It will cause an honest person to become a cheat. It will cause a faithful person to become a fraud. Like David one must confess his/her sin. It must be called what it is.

Conclusion

Is there hope of healing from the wound of infidelity? Yes, absolutely! Eighty-one percent of the couples who go to marriage therapy reconcile. 81%! But I do not mean one or two times. This is a long costly process. Three very important things will keep reconciliation from happening. The first is un-forgiveness. The meaning of the word forgiveness: must be made clear – nailed down. Many people will say to me, "I can't forget what he has done so I must not have forgiven him." Forgiving has nothing to do with forgetting. The Bible says, "God remembers our sin no more." (Hebrews 10-17) But we are not God! It is not healthy for us to forget even if we could. We need to remember how we are hurt so we can keep it from happening again. Do not put those two words together – forgiving and forgetting. "To forgive is to let go of any wish or desire to harm or to get even." When we come to the place of not wishing that person to be dead or wanting him to hurt as bad as I have then we have forgiven. To come to the place of forgiveness is a process. It is not an event. You cannot place a date or the time that forgiveness will take place. To be angry, to hurt or even hate is all a part of the process.

A minister's 14 year old daughter was raped and killed. The killer was in jail 3 days after and the minister went to the jail telling the man that he forgave him because he was a Christian. Thirty years later he is in my office working on his grief and forgiveness. He aborted the process. One must stay in the process for as long as it takes.

Secondly, the offender wants to talk about the affair and then never talk about it again. This cannot happen! It must stay open. You do not sew up a physical wound while there is infection on the inside. You put in a drain tube and let it heal from the inside out. So it is with an emotional wound. The offendee must be allowed to bring it up as long as she has questions or has a need to discuss it. There will come a time when it is not discussed any longer but it will come naturally and not be forced.

Thirdly, the couple must be careful in their discussions about the affair not to give details that will put pictures in the offendee's head that can never be removed. When former South Carolina Governor Mark Sanford confessed on national TV that his affair was "the love story of the century" I knew they would divorce. News Channel 19 in Columbia interviewed me that same night and I said so. Jenny Sandford later said, "I could never get that picture out of my mind."

To heal the couple must focus on rebuilding the trust broken. Trust is broken in an instant but it takes a process to rebuild it. That process takes note of the small acts of self-revelation. One must do what one says he will do and be where one says he will be. This process must be thought and talked about daily until trust is rebuilt. The marriage will never return to what it was because of the loss of innocence, but it can be much better than it was ever in the past.

I often see infidelity happening for one or two reasons: to end a marriage or to begin a marriage. If this wound has happened to you, may it result in beginning a marriage like you have dreamed of.

Let us pray.

Lord, this is a tragic story of desire, deception and death. Help us learn about this wound of infidelity that leaves a long path of broken hearts, failed dreams, uprooted children and disrupted families. In the process of our learning may we be healed from this wound and become healers to others dealing with this wound. May it be so. In Jesus' name. Amen.

May God bless you and keep you healing from your wounds.

WHAT HAPPENS TO US IS NOT THAT IMPORTANT.

IT IS WHAT HAPPENS TO WHAT HAPPENS TO US THAT IS IMPORTANT.

Alistair V. Campbell wrote, "the authority with which we offer help to others derives from our own acquaintance with grief...The wounded healer heals, because he or she is able to convey, as much by presences as by the words used, both an awareness and a transcendence of loss... Wounded healers heal because they, to some degree at least, have entered the depths of their own experiences of loss and in those depths found hope again."

(Rediscovering Pastoral Care, p 51)

CHAPTER 10

TAMAR: WOUNDED BY SEXUAL ABUSE

Text: 2 Samuel 13:1-22

CIT: *(Central Idea of the text)*
            Amnon raped his virgin sister Tamar.

Thesis: The wounds of childhood sexual abuse are the most difficult
            wounds to heal.

Purpose:

- Major Objective: Supportive
- Specific Objective: Through the power of the Holy Spirit,
  I hope to raise our awareness of and prayer for all who have
  suffered childhood sexual abuse.

Introduction

Outline:
    I.   The Wounder Is Filled With Lust and Power - vs. 1-14
    II.   The Wounder Is Filled With Self-Hate and Anger - vs. 15-17
    III.   The Wounded Are Powerless - vs. 12-14
    IV.   The Wounded Feels Disgraced - v. 13
    V.   The Wounded Feels the Loss and Grief - v. 19
    VI.   The Wounded Are Misunderstood and Mistreated - v. 20

Conclusion:

"Freedom
without maturity
will always
get us in trouble."

"Lust cannot wait
to get,
But love can wait
to give."

"There cannot be
a consenting child."

The Word of the Lord

2 Samuel 13:1-22

1 In the course of time Amnon, son of David, fell in love with Tamar, the beautiful sister of Absalom, another son of David.

2 Amnon became frustrated to the point of illness on account of his sister Tamar for she was a virgin and it seemed impossible for him to do anything to her.

3 Now, Amnon had a friend named Jonadab, son of Shammah, David's brother. Jonadab was a very shrewd man. 4 He asked Amnon, "Why do you the king's son look so haggard morning after morning? Won't you tell me?" Amnon said to him, "I'm in love with Tamar, my brother Absalom's sister."

5 "Go to bed and pretend to be ill," Jonadab said. "When your father comes to see you say to him, 'I would like my sister Tamar to come and give me something to eat. Let her prepare the food in my sight so I may watch her and then eat it from her hand.'"

6 So Amnon lay down and pretended to be ill when the king came to see him and said to him, "I'd like my sister Tamar to come and make some special bread in my sight so I might eat from her hand."

7 David sent word to Tamar at the palace. "Go to the house of your brother Amnon and prepare some food for him." 8 So Tamar went to the house of her brother Amnon who was lying down. She took some dough and kneaded it and made the bread in his sight and baked it. 9 Then she took the pan and served him the bread but he refused to eat. "Send everyone out of here," Amnon said. So everyone left. 19 Then Amnon said to Tamar, "Bring the food here into my bedroom so I may eat from your hand." Tamar took the bread she had prepared and brought it to her brother Amnon in his bedroom. 11 But when she took it to him to eat, he grabbed her and said, "Come to bed with me my sister."

12 "Don't, my brother," she said to him. "Don't force me. Such a thing should not be done in Israel. Don't do this wicked thing. 13 What about me? Where can I get rid of my disgrace? What about you? You would be like one of the wicked fools in Israel. Please speak to the king. He will not keep me from marrying you." 14 But he refused to listen to her. Since he was stronger than she, he raped her.

15 Then Amnon hated her with intense hatred. In fact he hated her more than he had loved her. Amnon said to her, "Get up and get out." 16 "No," she said to him. "Sending me away would be a greater wrong than what you've already done to me." But he refused to listen to her. 17 He called his personal servant and said, "Get this woman out of here and bolt the door after her." 18 So his servant put her out and bolted the door after her. She was wearing a richly ornate robe, for this was the kind of garment that the virgin daughters of the king wore. 19 Tamar put ashes on her head and tore the robe she was wearing. She put her hand on her head and went away weeping as loud as she went.

20 Her brother Absalom said to her, "Has that Amnon your brother been with you? Be quiet now my sister. He is your brother. Don't take this thing to heart." And Tamar lived in her brother Absalom's house a desolate woman.

21 When King David heard all this he was furious. 22 Absalom never said a word to Amnon either good or bad. He hated Amnon because he had disgraced his sister Tamar.

Introduction

Being raised by a widow with four children still in the home, a widow who was often unable to parent because she suffered from Brown Lung disease from a textile mill, being raised in that environment I had much, much more freedom than any child needed. Freedom without maturity will always get us in trouble.

As a nine-year-old usually about once a month I would take some earnings from my newspaper route and I would ride the Duke Power bus to Spartanburg and go to the Carolina Theater downtown. More often I would have one or more little friends with me but on this particular day I had none. It was my custom to go to the theater and spend my money on the ticket and popcorn and candy or I whatever I wanted to eat. Then I would hitchhike home 8 miles north of Spartanburg.

One Saturday as a nine-year-old I was picked up by two adult males whom I did not know, taken to a remote country road and sexually molested. It was a horrifying experience. Yet even today, I remember the trauma of that Saturday. Not understanding what was taking place but knowing that this could be fatal.

Childhood sex abuse is one of the most difficult wounds to ever heal. One of the most tragic wounds to deal with and if not dealt with in childhood, when it is dealt with it puts an adult in psychotherapy longer than any other wound. The research shows that the people who spend the longest amount of time in therapy are those who were sexually abused as children. One in four girls are sexually abused by the time they're fourteen. One in six boys are sexually abused by the time they're sixteen. What complicates these stats is that only one in ten childhood sexual abuse events is reported. One in ten! The research shows that today we have 39 + million adults in America dealing with childhood sexual abuse. Thirty-nine plus million. [28]

It is a wound that society should not accept. It is a wound that Christian people ought to be aware of. It is a wound that we ought to pray daily about. It is a wound that we should pray about everyday for those who are wounded.

The National Justice Institute reports that we spend $23 billion a year in America in physical and mental health for those wounded in this fashion. [29]

We have an horrific story in our text. One that I think we can learn greatly from. It is out of the tragic life of David, the tragic family life of David. He may have been an awesome king but he was a pitiful parent. He may have been a wonderful man, but he was a sorry dad. Many of the things he sowed in his life, he reaped through his family. Amnon is his first born son. Tamar is Absalom's sister. So, Tamar is Amnon's half sister. Different mother; same father. In our text it says Amnon falls in love with his virgin sister Tamar. We do not know how old she was. I suspect she was what we consider today a child. Because, at puberty they were considered adults. At puberty a girl was of marriageable age and often did marry. They had no long adolescent period in their culture unlike what we have in our culture. It did not exist. It still does

---

[28] http://www.scchildren.org/childrenstrust/aboutchildabuse.shtm/
[29] National Institute of Justice (Victim Cost and Consequences: A New Look, 1996)

not exist in many countries. So Tamar without doubt was a child in our calculations today.

The scripture says that Amnon fell in love with her. Let me correct that. What he experienced and what we have recorded in this text is not love. What we have recorded in this text is raw sexual lust. There is a difference. Parents and grandparents, you need to say to your children, "Here's the difference between these two 'L' words. Lust cannot wait to get but love can wait to give." Let that be that little precious daughter's mantra. Lust can not wait to get but love can wait to give.

Amnon is eaten up with it. His cousin recognizes his 'love moping.' Let me correct myself...his 'LUST moping' because he is not getting what he wants. He's horney and he has a beautiful sister and that's all he's got on his mind. So his cousin says, you don't need to be haggard all the time. You are the king's son. Being the king's son, you deserve anything you want. You deserve anything you need. Let me again reiterate. It is not love. It is lust.

Liberty Hill Presbyterian Church has defined love in such a way that it's been the most useful thing that we have ever done together in my practice. The definition goes like this: "To love you is to desire the absolute best for you," meaning to proactively desire the absolute best for you. That's love. That kind of thinking did not enter in Amnon's mind at all. He wanted what he wanted when he wanted it. He didn't give one rip about Tamar.

A number of years ago I was assigned a pedophile by a judge in Camden. It was the first pedophile I had ever worked with. I did not want to work with him because I still had some unresolved stuff from my own experience. Rather than council him, I wanted to kill him. But I took the case because I felt like this could be useful in my own journey of healing and it very much was. I worked with this person for months. He had sexually abused both of his daughters. He took one of them across the state line so it was a federal case. Never once could I get him to admit he was a pedophile. Never once could I get him to admit he had done a wrong thing. He was teaching his daughters how to be good wives because he loved them so much.

Usually they subpoena my testimony but in his court case being in Virginia they just asked for a letter. I wrote a scorching letter. He received thirty-seven years.

It is not love that causes one to do that. It is lust and power. Lust and power. And Amnon is eaten up with it. So he devises this plan with the help of his cousin, making him as guilty as he is. Tamar brings him some homemade bread, bakes it in his presence. He coaxes her into feeding him in the bed and there he overpowers her and rapes her.

"Well, preacher, was she just stupid to go into his bedroom?"

It's her brother! We too quickly judge those who have been wounded in this fashion.

"Well, she shouldn't wear what she wears. Have you seen what revealing clothes she wears?"

It doesn't matter if she's running nude! It's not a child's fault. There is no equal power within a child. There can not be a consenting child. Ever! It was not Tamar's fault. No, she wasn't stupid. She was ministering to her brother and he grabs her. I want you to see in the midst of that horrific threat how beautiful she was in her response. How brilliantly and intelligent her response was. She says "Don't do this wicked thing. What you are about to do is a wicked thing in Israel. Please do not do this wicked thing, Amnon." She appeals to his conscious. Do you not have a little voice within you that is saying this is wrong? Do not do this, please. But, that is to no avail. He will not listen. His conscious is not there.

They didn't have the term sociopath in those days but we have it in our day. Many of our offenders are sociopaths. No social conscious. So, she appeals to something that was not there. He would not listen. It did not matter. So, she goes to compassion. If conscious does not work, perhaps compassion will. Do you realize what you are doing to me? Do not disgrace me in this fashion. But, he has no compassion. She's tried his conscious and found it void. She tried his compassion and found it missing.

Then she appeals to his conceit. I guess she figured since he did not have any compassion, he's without conscious, maybe the deceitful fool will listen. She says to him, "Do not become one of the fools in Israel. Think about yourself. You don't care if this is wicked. You don't care about me. Think about your narcissistic self. Do you want to be one of the fools like exist in Israel?" Then she tries this brilliant stall. She says to him, "Let's go to the king. The king can do anything. Let's say to him that we are in love. Surely, he will allow us to be together." That was a stall. David wouldn't have it. Levitical law would not allow marrying your sister or half sister. David would not have done that. She knew that but she was stalling, hoping that the conscious statement, the compassion statement, the conceit statement - maybe it will work. But, it didn't. And he raped her.

Did you notice the line after that? After he had sex with his sister, the scripture says his hatred for her was more than his love was for her. His lust was satisfied. Now get out. She said, what can I tell them? I'm a disgraced woman. A defiled woman. Where can I go? There's no place for people like me to go. Please let me stay. Don't make the end worse than what it already is.

He forced her to leave and bolted the door behind her. Love? Not by any definition I've ever heard. Not even care. No concern at all. She leaves weeping, throwing her brilliant colored robes over her head, tearing them, finding ashes, pouring them over her head and her face, ritualistically saying, "I am deeply grieved." Absalom, her brother, really did love her. He only had one daughter. He named her Tamar. He did love her but he was not wrong about something like this. So, he really doesn't have to hear what happened. He knows what happened. He says to her, and this is awful, "Be quiet. Don't say anything about this. This is a family matter."

Did you hear what he said? Thirty to 45% of the childhood sexual abuse is done by a family member. You wonder why only one in ten is reported? DON'T MESS UP OUR FAMILY! You don't want to embarrass us all over the church! All over the community. Keep this quite. Suffer patiently and in silence.

She's just been abused and now she's being abused again. He says to her, did you hear it, "This is no big matter." One of the worst wounds that a person can experience! "This is no big matter!" You move into my house and keep your mouth shut. Suck it up. Get over this. It's no big matter. She lives... did you catch that word?... as a desolate woman the rest of our life.

I have never talked with an adult person of sexual abuse as a child that did not feel as if they were dirty. That they were damaged goods. I remember talking to a client who had a medical background. She said, "When I have that flashback today my flesh crawls." I said, "Be aware of something. You're in the medical field. You above anyone else knows this to be true. The skin you have today is not the skin he touched as a child." She was like, "Wow! That's true. We slough it off everyday." We don't have that picture that the reptile has when he just crawls out of his in one big swoop. We drop ours everyday, every minute. The skin you had then, you do not have now. The skin you have now, he's never touched.

Horrible wound to deal with. Horrible wound to get over. One we need to be mindful of and with 30 to 45% of it taking place in the family, don't ever believe it can't happen in your family. Don't ever believe it can't happen to your grandchildren. Don't ever believe that. It can and it does happen to the most wealthy families, to the poorest, to the most educated families, to the most ignorant. There is no family... there is no family... this cannot happen to. Be aware with your little ones, on guard with your little ones. Pray for your little ones.

What we now know from an 18-month study with the Medical University of Charleston that was just finished, childhood sexual trauma, when dealt with within 6 months to a year, can be alleviated with 12 to 14 sessions of therapy. Whereas, if you carry that with you as an adult into adulthood, disassociated and repressed, it often takes years of therapy to work through. This is something we need to be mindful of and pray for.

I said Absalom was stupid. David was stupider. Is that a word? He was more stupid. David hears about this and does not say one word to Amnon, his eldest son. Absalom does not speak to him for two years. David does not address that family friction at all. Zero. Two years later Absalom has been seething over this - two years - and he says to his father, "I ask you to allow all the King's sons to go down to the party at the sheep shearing event down in the valley." David does question that but he lets them all go. Absalom says to his men, "When I tell you to strike him, you strike him dead." Two years later Absalom killed his brother Amnon. No family reconciliation. No family discussion. No family healing. They just go on to be wounded wounders.

Conclusion

A high percentage of those who abuse children were abused as a child. Wounded wounders, not wounded healers. We can be wounded healers; wounded healers within our own lives with our own wounds or wounded healers for those around us in communities and in families of faith. But first, we must deal with our own wounds. We must find healing within ourselves, healing within our relationship to the one who said, "By my stripes, by my lashes you are healed." We have one, our Creator, who loved us so much he came and lived and was wounded to death on our behalf and extends to us an invitation "to bring our wounds to him." In our healing we can comrade together to be sources of healing for other people.

The Zen student came to the teacher and said, "I have nothing in my hands to bring." The teacher said, "Put it down." And the student said, "I don't have anything to put down." And then the teacher said, "Well then carry it on with you." There are those who say I'm not wounded. I don't have any wounds in my hand. Okay. Then carry them on.

But there's another possibility and that is to bring those wounds to the feet of the one who was wounded for you and say, "Lord, here they are." Here's how I've been hurt. Will you take that hurt and that pain and help me to heal? May it be true for you today.

Let us pray.

Oh Lord, thank you that in your scriptures you just present the good, bad, and ugly. Life is lived as it is. At times, in all of its dysfunctional families as David's, it's rape, it's murder. All the mayhem of life is in your Word. Thank you. Help us to know in the midst of this murder and mayhem, rape and family dysfunction that you stand with outstretched nail-scarred hands saying to us, "I offer you healing." Help us oh God to acknowledge our wounds to you, accept your healing forgiveness, and help us to truly heal that we may be wounded healers. May it be so. In Jesus' name. Amen.

God bless you and keep you healing.

WHAT HAPPENS TO US IS NOT THAT IMPORTANT.

**IT IS WHAT HAPPENS TO WHAT HAPPENS
TO US THAT IS IMPORTANT.**

Bill Wilson (1895-1971) was wounded by alcoholism. His grandfather was also an alcoholic. In 1933 at age 38 he hit bottom spending days and nights in a constant alcoholic stupor. He met Dr. Robert Smith who was in the same condition. They became healers for each other and together they formed "Alcoholics Anonymous." Today it is the number one approach in getting one sober and keeping one in recovery. Over 2 million members in over 150 countries claim that it is healing them from alcoholism.

CHAPTER 11

A WOMAN: WOUNDED BY SICKNESS

Text: Luke 8:43-48

CIT: *(Central Idea of the text)*
            A woman, wounded by a chronic sickness, touched Jesus
            and was instantly healed

Thesis: Jesus is not physically present to be touched by the wounded
            but we are.

Purpose:

   • Major Objective: Evangelistic
   • Specific Objective: Through the power of the Holy Spirit,
     I hope to lead each of us into becoming wounded healers.

Introduction

Outline:
   I.   Wounded By Her Disease - vs. 43; Mark 5:26
   II.   Wounded By The Disease Caused Isolation - vs. Leviticus
         15:19-33
   III. Wounded By The Disease's Longevity - Mark 5:25-26;
         Luke - 8:43
   IV.   Wounded Becomes Healer - Luke 8:48; Mark 5:33-34

Conclusion: "Only the deepest wounds that leave no visible scars make
            a healer out of the wounded." (Frank, J. Persuasion and
            Healing, 1974)

"We are living in an age
where we do not have to blame
everything that happens
on God.
We know there are viruses.
We know there are diseases.
We know there are
genetically transmitted diseases that have
nothing whatsoever to do with God.
Yet we continue
to lay it
at God's doorstep."

The Word of the Lord

Luke 8: 43–48

As Jesus was on his way, the crowds almost crushed him. 43 And a woman was there who had been subject to bleeding for twelve years, but no one could heal her. 44 She came up behind him and touched the edge of his cloak, and immediately her bleeding stopped.

45 "Who touched me?" Jesus asked. When they all denied it, Peter said, "Master, the people are crowding and pressing against you."

46 But Jesus said, "Someone touched me; I know that power has gone out from me."

47 Then the woman, seeing that she could not go unnoticed, came trembling and fell at his feet. In the presence of all the people, she told why she had touched him and how she had been instantly healed. 48 Then he said to her, "Daughter, your faith has healed you. Go in peace."

Introduction

Mrs. Smith called the doctor about her husband's illness and the doctor said to her, "Mrs. Smith, I've said to you before Mr. Smith is fine. I just did a physical with him last week. He just thinks he's sick. It's in his head. He just thinks he's sick."

She goes back two weeks later. The doctor sees Mrs. Smith and he asks her, "Well, how's Mr. Smith?" She said, "Things have gotten worse. He now thinks he's dead."

All of us, I believe, worry when we are sick. All of us at some point in time and to some degree, become sick. But really when we're sick there's only two things to worry about. You're either going to get better and, if you do, there's nothing to worry about. Or you're going to get worse. If you get worse there's only two things to worry about. You either eventually are going to get better or you're going to die. If you die there's only two things to worry about. You're either going to Heaven or you're going to Hell. If you go to Heaven there's nothing to worry about. If you go to Hell you won't worry. You'll be too busy greeting all your old friends, so really we shouldn't be worrying when we are sick.

117

Sickness is a wound that comes to all of us. To some degree, in some form, sickness is a wound that touches us all.

In our story we did not talk about the beginning part of the story. So let me place it in context. Jesus is on his way to a synagogue ruler's house. The synagogue ruler was named Jarius. Jarius comes to Jesus and says, "My little 12 year old daughter is sick unto death. Please come and help her." Jesus is on his way to Jarius' house to heal this rich, very important, very popular ruler's daughter.

In our story the woman is unnamed, sick and outcast and financially broke. So we have represented two wide spectrums of life. One who is very wealthy, very well recognized in the community, a lot of political clout and power, a lot of religious prestige, recognition and power. The other end of the spectrum is a woman who is not even named, who has been an outcast for 12 years.

Disease is like that. Disease touches all of us, in all stations, positions of life. All of us. Sooner or later this thing called disease will be the vehicle that takes us out of life as we know it, unless of course we are tragically taken out by some unexpected accident or act of terrorism.

Disease is as much a part of life as life itself. Those of you who've been with me for a while have heard me say this numerous times but it bears repeating because it is so popular. When we come down with disease as did this woman, as many of you are dealing with right now, it is not a visitation from God. God does not give us cancer to get our attention. God does not take away one of our eyes to see how we're going to react today. God does not do that kind of stuff.

I was talking to one of you this morning who's reading Richard Dawkins, who is an agnostic. Actually, he's more than an agnostic. He's an atheist. Bob says to me that Richard Dawkins is one of the most brilliant atheists he's ever read. I would agree. I've read everything Richard Dawkins has written. I said the problem with Richard Dawkins is, he only knows one kind of Christian. One kind. That's all. The only Christian he knows is a Fundamentalist. He does not know, probably never met, a progressive liberal, 18th century Enlightenment thinker about Christianity. He criticizes only one form. I am not of that form. [30]

We are living in an age where we do not have to blame everything

---

[30] Dawkins, Richard. *The God Delusion.* Boston: Mariner Books. 2006

that happens on God. We know there are viruses. We know there are diseases. We know there are genetically transmitted diseases that have nothing whatsoever to do with God. Yet we continue to lay it at God's doorstep. Since I do so much therapy with people, there is a deep psychological problem with that. When I blame God for the disease that I have, God gave it to me for some unknown reason. How is it that I go to God and find comfort, hope and encouragement? God did it to me.

There is this little girl just getting over the mumps. She's a PK - preacher's kid. Her preacher father says to her, "As we're praying let us thank God for taking your mumps away and healing you." But she said, "Wait Daddy. Did he not give them to me?" Out of the mouths of babes.

It is very, very difficult for us if you'll just think through it. It is very difficult for us to come to God in those times of a health crisis if there is a part of us that believes God gave me this to somehow test my faith, to somehow find out what I'm made of. If God knows all things God knows what I'm made of to begin with. It is not God. It is disease.

This woman comes to Jesus with her disease. How could she have touched him if she believed he gave it to her. Would she have faith to have done that? Not at all. Life is filled with diseases. I'm now reading that by the time we are age 30, everyone of us is carrying cancer viruses within us. It just depends on how active and fortified our immune system is as to whether or not we're going to be able to fight that off or whether it's going to settle in some part of ourselves. When we take God out of the equation of disease and believe that disease is just a part of life, then we have someone, like this woman, who we can go to. Here she is wounded with this disease of bleeding. Exactly what her condition was we don't know. She is pressing in this crowd hoping to get close enough to Jesus not to touch him because she won't do that. She has not been able to touch anyone for 12 years because of Leviticus 15. Her disease is not only taxing her body it is taxing her spirit and her soul. No one can touch her. She is unclean according to the scriptures. No one can touch her and she can touch no one. Anything that she touches must be washed; not only just washed but washed ceremonially.

I know just a little bit about that kind of dread and isolation. My mother had Brown Lung disease from the textile mill but they only found out what it was in 1955. Up until that point she had been treated for tuberculosis. You know what they do when you had tuberculosis in the old days. They isolate you. I remember not being able to sit in her lap. Not being able to kiss her or receive a kiss from her. I remember utensils in the kitchen that she had set aside for her and her only. I remember all too well the first time they put her away. That was the form of treatment at that time. They would put you away in a very pastoral kind of place with sun, trees and flowers and hope that the rest, just the rest, would bring you healing. I remember the first time. I remember riding my bicycle and walking down the back side of those apartments looking in the windows trying to see her. I remember that kind of isolation.

Here is a woman, because of Leviticus scriptures, has not been touched in 12 years. Nor has she touched anyone for 12 years. She is so aware of that, she is not going to try to touch Jesus. All she is going to do is attempt to touch his clothes. She believes that if she can just touch his clothes, she will be healed.

I regret deeply the situation that we are in today when it comes to touching in our society. I regretted the day about 15 years ago when I received my personal liability insurance and it had a statement, a question on there, "Do you in your practice of psychotherapy ever have a reason to touch a client? If you do, explain fully." I thank God for the privilege of shaking your hand and hugging you, embracing you as people of faith because I can't do that with clients anymore. There is a very powerful healing in touch, but you can't do that anymore because it can be misunderstood. If you're taken to the courts they will not find it in your favor. The courts will assume where there is smoke there is fire. Therefore, the powerful healing potential of touch I cannot do with my clients.

We live in a sad day when it comes to that. We were moving in that day when Paul said a long time ago, greet each other with a holy kiss. Well, we had stopped doing that because the kisses became unholy. They have progressively gotten more unholy in the society of which we are apart.

Here is a woman suffering from a disease 12 years and all three of the synoptic gospels tell us 12 years. It's interesting to me the way they used to write things down. Before they wrote things down they had it in oral form. They remembered it orally. Transmitted it orally so they created it in such a fashion they could remember it. So here is a little girl. How old is she? Twelve. She dies and Jesus touches her and she resurrects. Then, here is a woman who is sick for how long? Twelve years. Whether that's historically absolutely correct or not we don't know. It doesn't matter because that's the way they put it in an oral form to remember and transmit stories to each other until the point of time when they were written down.

So here is a woman. Her sickness has been long -12 years. Luke we believe was a physician so he says nothing about her trials and tribulations. Nothing. Mark on the other hand, who is not a physician tells us that this woman has suffered much at the hands of doctors. They just can't figure out what's wrong exactly. Second, Mark says that she has spent all of her livelihood trying to find healing for this disease. Third, Mark says she is no better. She is worse. Twelve years. Frustrated by the physicians. Broke financially and her condition is worsening. Get that picture? And in the midst of this host of people gathered around Jesus, this woman believes her faith is of such if she can just touch his clothes. I don't have to touch him. That would not be lawful. I can't ask him to touch me. That would not be lawful. All I need to do is to touch his clothes. If I can just touch his garment then I'll be healed. She did and she was.

Knowing that something had taken place Jesus asks, "Who touched me?" Did you hear his disciples? "What kind of question is that? You got people bumping and shoving and pushing and everything else. They're all over you. What do you mean, 'Who touched me?'"

Jesus said, "No. I've just experienced the loss of power. Someone was healed." And she comes and falls at his feet and confesses. This marvelous statement he says to her, "My daughter, your faith has healed you." Your faith has healed you.

Let me be a little critical at this point of those who are in the professional healing ministry who use this as a way out. If you come to them and you're not healed, it's not their fault. It's your faith. You do not have the faith to be healed. So they're always protected and always in the clear. If you are healed, well, they kind of want to take the glory.

But if you aren't healed, it's your fault because you don't have the faith. I could wish that if we had the faith all of us could be healed. That's just not the way life is. All of us are going to be exposed to an unhealed disease that will become the vehicle that carries us to Glory. It's just that simple. If a disease does not take us to meet Jesus, then some tragic accident will. But it is the disease that is the vehicle that will take us out of this life as we know it and take us to be with our Lord.

How can we find healing, spiritual healing, in the context of no physical healing? This lady found physical healing but I think all of us can find healing, meaning we can come to the place of acceptance, the place of embracing, and the place of even thriving in the disease that is going to take us out of this life into the life beyond. The first step in doing that is to not place this disease at the feet of God. Place the disease where it belongs - in the realm of life and health and disease. When we truly believe that this is just a part of life and that I have someone in the Lord whom I can touch and who will touch me and will help me to be spiritually, holistically healed in the context of not being healed physically, we will have come a long way.

Conclusion

I deal with those and have for many, many years, who go out of this life fighting every single breath with every ounce of energy they have. It's a losing battle because something is going to take us away. To embrace something as a vehicle that is simply a vehicle to take us away, is very much part of our healing. The Greek word for salvation is Sozo and that word literally means to be bound together in such a way that we are whole. Sickness, disease will shatter us from within if we allow it but if we have the faith to take God by the hand and with the Spirit's help, we can walk through these days of disease until the point that it takes us home. Can you see that as a form of healing? Can you embrace that as a form of healing? It is a journey we are all going to take sooner or later at some point in time. Fight it and live as long and as healthy as we can, yes. Deny it as a part of life's existence and we'll lose. Lose tragically. I believe we can be healed in the presence of our wound. We can be healed in the presence of our sickness. We can be healed in the presence of our dying when we reach out and find a health in our Creator that is there. But notice, Jesus did not reach out to her. She reached out to him. And he said, "Daughter your faith has made you whole."

You know where you are today in your need of healing, your need of wholeness. You know where you are today. What's preventing you from reaching out and touching the one who can make you whole?

Let us pray.

Oh Lord, thank you for this marvelous story, this story of healing. We could wish that all of our stories could end in this fashion, but they cannot. They did not even in this woman's life. Some other disease took her out of this planet. So it will be with us. Help us to know in the midst of our struggle with sickness and disease that you are in the midst of that struggle with us. If we will reach out and touch you, you are present to make us whole to live with and to be victorious through our illnesses and our wound. Then this woman became a testimony possibly helping someone else. Help us not to be wounded wounderers. Depressed, disgusted. Angry and hostile because of our wounds. Help us to find healing and then become instruments of healing to others. May it be so. In Jesus' name. Amen.

May God bless you and keep you healing.

WHAT HAPPENS TO US IS NOT THAT IMPORTANT.

IT IS WHAT HAPPENS TO WHAT HAPPENS TO US THAT IS IMPORTANT.

Charles Joseph Whitman was born June 24, 1941 in Lake Worth, FL. He has been called America's first "mass murderer" as the infamous "Texas Tower Sniper."

Some wounded are doomed to become wounders having no choice to become healers. Such is the case with Charles Whitman when on August 1, 1966 he climbed the tower of the University of Texas and shot 17 people to death and wounded 32 others. His autopsy revealed he had both a tumor and a vascular malformation pressing against his amygdale, the small and primitive region of the brain that controls emotions.

Time Life: Inside the Criminal Mind – Understanding How Bad People Think, p. 28

CHAPTER 12

JUDAS: WOUNDED BY DISAPPOINTMENT

Text: Matthew 26:47-50; 27:1-5

CIT: *(Central Idea of the text)* Judas, filled with grief and guilt for betraying Jesus, hanged himself.

Thesis: When we fail to heal from our wounds we become wounded wounders.

Purpose:
- Major Objective: Supportive
- Specific Objective: Through the power of the Holy Spirit, I hope to lead each of us in being healed and becoming healers.

Introduction

Outline:
  I.   Wounded By Disappointment In Jesus' Person - v. 27:4
  II.   Wounded By Disappointment In Jesus' Purpose - v. 27:3
  III. Wounded Wounder - v. 27:5

Conclusion:

"To harbor, sit with, massage,
to entertain saying
time and time again
those words, those actions
of disappointment,
will be no help to you.
They will not help you.
They will only deepen your
wound of disappointment
in that spouse.
They will only cause you to look for
and expect other disappointments."

*"Marriages are made
in the
blood, sweat and tears
of everyday
forgiveness. . ."*

The Word of the Lord

Matthew 26:47-50

47 While he was still speaking, Judas, one of the Twelve arrived. With him was a large crowd armed with swords and clubs, sent from the chief priests and elders of the people. 48 Now the betrayer had arranged the signal with them: "The one I kiss is the man; arrest him." 49 Going at once to Jesus, Judas said, "Greetings, Rabbi!" and kissed him."

50 Jesus replying, "Friend, do what you came for."

Matthew 27:1-5

1 Early in the morning, all the chief priests and the elders of the people came to the decision to put Jesus to death. 2 They bound him, led him away and handed him over to Pilate, the governor.

3 When Judas, who had betrayed him, saw that Jesus was condemned, he was seized with remorse and returned the 30 silver coins to the chief priests and the elders. 4 "I have sinned," he said, "for I have betrayed innocent blood." "What is that to us?" they replied. "That's your responsibility."

5 So Judas threw the money into the temple and left. Then he went away and hanged himself."

Introduction

What is done, is done. It cannot be undone. William Barclay wrote: "the moving finger writes; and having writ, moves on; nor all thy piety nor wit shall lure it back to cancel half a line, nor all thy tears wash out a word of it." [31]

How many of you have a father, a brother, an uncle, or some male back there in your family with the name Judas? Let's see your hand? Anyone? Let's see the hands of those of you who have named a pet dog, cat, or a goldfish Judas. Let's see your hand. Not a single hand. Jesus was right. Jesus told Judas you will be cursed for generations to come. That's recorded in the Gospel of Judas. It is not a gospel that made it

---

[31] Barclay, William. The Gospel of Matthew: Philadelphia: The Westminister Press, 1957. Vol. 2, p. 372

into our Canon of scripture. But in 180AD the church father Arthenius condemned the Gospel of Judas as heresy and forbade its preaching, teaching, and reciting in any of the churches. So we know that the gospel was around in 180AD and was condemned by the church. For 1600 years it was unheard of. Most of those Gospels that did not make it into the Canon were burned, destroyed, and those that were saved were often hidden away somewhere in a cave, as was the Gospel of Judas.

The Gospel of Judas was found by a farmer in middle Egypt on the right side of the Nile River not far from the town of Ambar. It was discovered in 1978. It made the circuit through the antique dealers for a number of years much to its destruction. When it came to linguistics on July 24, 2001, it was discovered truly what they had. In over four thousand pieces it was tenaciously under microscope put back together. We have it in English print today, The Gospel According to Judas. [32]

In that Gospel Jesus thanks Judas for carrying out his role in Jesus's destiny. It's a little different twist from what we have received. It is not believed that Judas wrote the Gospel although some argue that he did. But it is not likely since our text tells us that right after his condemnation, Judas hanged himself.

When you think about Judas and why this happened and how it happened, one has several options to take. One may consider Judas as a victim. Someone had to betray Jesus. Psalm 41:9 said and I quote, "Even my close friend whom I trusted, he who shared my bread, has lifted his heel against me." So someone close to Jesus in order to fulfill prophecy, had to betray him. There are those who say Judas was simply a victim of fate. Someone had to do it and Judas was the one chosen.

And there are those who take another position which is very, very close to this position and that is that Judas was simply a robot. No will, no integrity of his own. He was simply a robot in the hands of Satan to do this task of betraying Jesus.

Then there are those who take the position that Judas was an apostate, meaning he fell from Grace. It is not a Baptist position; they believe in "once saved, always saved." Nor is it a Presbyterian position who like to talk about the "Elect." If you are the elect, I don't think you

---

[32] Kasser. Rodolphe; Meyer, Marvin; and Wurst, Gregor, Eds. The Gospel of Judas, Washington, D.C.: National Geographic, 2006.

can become the un-elect. So, these two denominations would definitely not take this apostate position.

Then there are those who say, "No, Judas was never one of the Twelve. Only in appearance." His heart was never there. His heart was in the treasury bag. Judas was the treasurer and it does appear that he might have been a person of greed for he chastises the woman who breaks the bottle of very expensive perfume and anoints Jesus' feet. Judas chastises her and says we could have used that to feed the poor. Some would suggest he did not have the poor on his mind.

I take a different position. It is not a lone-wolf position. Long ago Thomas Pensonde de Quincey (1785-1850) of England, a British theologian, wrote extensively about this position and defended it aggressively as the only way to accept what Judas did. I wouldn't go that far. I think many positions would be viable but this is my position. I ask not that you agree but that you simply hear me. I didn't create this position just to fit in with the wounded healer series. I have believed this for a long, long time.

I believe Judas was wounded so severely by disappointment that he did what he did. Judas, without debate, was a Zealot. Peter, James, and John were also Zealots. Zealots were a group of people who believed the Messiah was coming...the Jewish Messiah. When the Jewish Messiah came, they were going to throw off the yoke of Roman opposition. They were going to once again become a nation even superior to the time of David. These men ate, slept and drank this hope of once again being an independent nation, claiming their gifts from God.

Judas was one of those and I believe that as these three years progressed through, toward the end of Jesus' ministry, Judas became more and more, increasingly disappointed in Jesus' purpose. More than that, Jesus' person. In relationship to his purpose, Judas saw him moving toward, not a physical uprising, not the establishment of a physical kingdom here on Earth. He kept talking about the kingdom of God within you. Judas did not want a kingdom of God within him. He wanted the kingdom of God in Jerusalem.

Jesus kept talking about this spiritual stuff, not the physical nuts and bolts of throwing off the yoke of opposition by the Roman government and ceasing to pay their outrageous taxes. Let us build the Kingdom here - blood, brick, and mortar. Judas believed Jesus was the Messiah and he would do it.

As he watched his purpose fade away he became disappointed. In fact I believe disappointed to the point of being wounded by his disappointment. Then I believe it took a deeper turn and Judas became disappointed in Jesus' person. Not just the mission, his ministry. His purpose was not in line with Judas's purpose. His very person was not in line. He was forgiving, merciful, graceful, accepting. "Render unto Caesar what is Caesar's and render unto God what is God's," as he held a coin in his hand with Caesar's portrait carved on it. I can imagine that galled Judas. "Render unto Caesar nothing! He deserves nothing! They are an occupying force. This Is Our God-given land. Kill Them All!"

Judas was disappointed. I can even imagine and this is out of my imagination that one of the Roman Centurions may well have slapped a Jewish face and then seeing so, Jesus said, "If thy enemy slaps you on one cheek, turn the other." I can see Judas seething inside. "Turn nothing!" Yet, I believe that there was a spark in Judas. A spark of hope in the midst of the discouragement. That if really pushed, this man who raised the dead, healed the sick, fixed crooked backs, made eyes to see, if really pushed, he would do something drastic and dramatic. "Let's push the envelope."

I believe that out of that deep disappointment, yet clinging to that little spark of hope, Judas goes to them and says, "I'll point him out for you. I'll name him, and I'll name him with a kiss."

Ever heard of the Judas kiss today? That sign of false affection. And the Judas slip which is a hole in the wall or room where someone is spied upon. We are all kin to Judas. All of us have been disappointed. All of us. All of us in our lives have been wounded by disappointment of persons and sometimes purposes.

I have been deeply involved in ministry, PTSD kind of ministry, to an Iraq veteran who believes so deeply it often scares me, that America's foreign policy has gone awry. He's a 27-year Marine veteran. He is disappointed in the purpose.

All of us from time to time are disappointed. You may be one of those who were in some ways disappointed with your parents. Hopefully you have come to that place where you acknowledge that they simply did the best they could do with what they had to do with. It might be that some of you come to that place where, 'well they were wounded, also.'

It was quite a realization to me one day - I'm so simple things come hard and slow. I had this realization that my parents had parents, too. Hello? Shocking! I would hope if that is a wound you have had to deal with, that you dealt with it sufficiently. Holding that wound, wallowing in the pus of that wound of disappointment about your parents and what your parents did or didn't do, will get you nowhere.

I won't name the movie. I don't want to ruin it for you but the whole movie is around this one statement that is so filled with passion. This young man says to his father, "I am sorry I disappointed you by not being the man that you are." The father said, "I am disappointed that you tried." I find that there are those who have spent so many years, so many years of disappointment at what their parents did not do, maybe could have done, but did not do, or did and wish they had not. It may be that one of you who have had disappointment, not in your parents, but in your child where you poured hopes and dreams and finances and everything else into the life of that child, and that child has been a wound. "I'm disappointed." How long will you nurse the wound? Will you allow the wound to so wound you that you in turn become a wounded wounder?

There are those times where we need to come to the place recognizing this child has will and volition of his or her own. "I did all that I could do, the best that I could do and I can no longer embrace this disappointment and how it continually wounds me."

It may be that you have a wound from a spouse. If you're married, you have a wound from a spouse. I don't care who you are! I say to the newlyweds that I marry today, "The vows you are now making, you'll break. The promises you're making you won't keep." Marriages are not made in Heaven. That's a lie. Marriages are made in the blood, sweat and tears of everyday forgiveness again and again and again because we wound each other. The only ones I know that do not wound each other is "he lives his life, she lives her life;" every once in awhile they have dinner together and every once in a while go to bed and have sex. Then you are not going to have wounds in an arrangement like that. But in my definition that's not a marriage.

To harbor, to sit with, to massage, to entertain saying time and time again those words, those actions of disappointment, will be no help to you. They will not help you. They will only deepen your wound of disappointment in that spouse. They will only cause you to look for and expect other disappointments.

It just may be that your job has disappointed you so greatly. You expected so much. Our youngest son has been with this company for 15 years. He was the person who went out to find new locations and new sites. He planned and carried out all of the updating and remodeling. After 15 years he had hopes of much higher callings with that company. They came to him and said we're not going to build anymore. We're not going to do any more remodeling for at least five years. Therefore, we don't need you. Do you nurse that kind of disappointment? What good does it do for you to nurse it, massage it? Let it go. Life is filled with disappointment.

As an eighteen year old, I stood in front of a Baptist minister in his home. At my side was clearly a very expectant bride. He married us. Five years later dealing with the mumps in my home I came to a faith commitment. That minister baptized me. For years he was a very important mentor in my life but I disappointed him. You know it's just not a good thing for a Baptist to become a Presbyterian in some circles. And, yes, he disappointed me. For over 25 years we have not had any contact whatsoever. Last night I had a dream, in fact many of them. It was disturbing. In this dream he and I were doing a worship service together. He's in his late 90s and still alive. In that worship service that we were doing together he was as tender, friendly and compassionate toward me as he had been in those early years. I awoke feeling good about that dream and with this goal in mind. I will send him a copy of today's tape with a letter stating that we disappointed each other.

But there is a greater disappointment than him. I grew up with the belief that God was the Alpha and the Omega, the first and the last. I grew up being taught that God was the author and the finisher of life. If you died, you died according to God's will, no matter what it was. If you were born you were born in God's will no matter what the circumstances. Like a fourteen-year-old in the backseat of a car under a beautiful full moon. It didn't matter. God was there causing it. I grew up that way. Therefore, when my 42 year old father died at home with a massive myocardial infarction, the word I used a little stronger was

God killed my father. For many years I was grievously disappointed in a God that would take the provider and plunge that household into deep, deep poverty.

I later learned that God had nothing to do with his heart attack. It was what was called heart disease. It just may be for years you have carried some serious disappointment in God's mercy or lack thereof in your life. I have persons say to me, "I prayed about this marriage. I prayed about this marriage. God didn't fix it!" No, and he won't. You'll have to. With God's help and God's strength you'll have to.

Conclusion

The deepest disappointment, the most destructive disappointment is the kind of disappointment that Judas harbored. A disappointment in God's purpose and person through the life of Jesus the Christ. One of the most tender moments I believe in John's Gospel is in the 15th chapter of John, when they're in the upper room observing the Lord's Supper. As tradition, Jesus took a sop of bread and wiped it through the gravy and handed it to Judas. What an act of Grace. What an act of appeal. Judas took the sop from the hands of his Lord and left. As he left, Jesus said to him, "What you must do, do quickly." How different Judas' life could have been had he dealt with that disappointment. Had he sat with his Lord and described how disappointed he was in his purpose and in his person. You may need to do it with your Lord, with your spouse, with your parents, with your child. For the wound of disappointment is a severe one. If unattended it will create within you a wounded wounder.

Let us pray.

Oh Lord, we confess that we do not know the heart of Judas. We do not know what compelled him to do what he did. But if he was gravely disappointed, we know what that means. Everyone of us here today has tasted the bitter gall of disappointment. Everyone of us here today has had persons disappointed in us. We may well carry that disappointment to the grave as did Judas. Or we can bring that disappointment to our Wounded Healer who, on Calvary's tree bore our stripes and by his wounds we are healed. May it be so. In Jesus' name. Amen.

May God bless you and keep you taking your wounds to the Cross.

WHAT HAPPENS TO US IS NOT THAT IMPORTANT.

**IT IS WHAT HAPPENS TO WHAT HAPPENS
TO US THAT IS IMPORTANT.**

Ram Dass and Paul Gorman have said, "We work on ourselves… in order to help others. And we help others as a vehicle for working on ourselves."

Ram Dass & Gorman, P. (1985). <u>How Can I Help?</u> New York: Alfred A. Knopf.

How have you been wounded?

CHAPTER 13

ZACCHAEUS: WOUNDED BY GREED & HEALED

Text: Luke 19:1-10

CIT: *(Central Idea of the text)*
             Wounded by greed Zacchaeus had collaborated with the
             Romans and worked himself up to a prominent position.

Thesis: Greed will wound us but it is not an incurable wound.

Purpose:
             • Major Objective: Evangelistic
             • Specific Objective: Through the power of the Holy Spirit,
               I hope to lead each of us in being healed from our selfish
               wounds.

Introduction

Outline:
    I.   Wounded By Greed - v. 2
    II.   Healed Of Greed - vs. 3-6
    III.   Wounded Healer - vs. 8-10

Conclusion:

"Whatever consumes
our greatest energy
then has become our God."

"Greed is an attitude."

"It is the love of money
that becomes the root
of all evil,
not money itself."

The Word of the Lord

Luke 19:1-10

Jesus entered Jericho and was passing through. 2 A man was there by the name of Zacchaeus; he was a chief tax collector and was wealthy. 3 He wanted to see who Jesus was but being a short man he could not, because of the crowd. 4 So he ran ahead and climbed a sycamore-fig tree to see him, since Jesus was coming that way.

5 When Jesus reached the spot, he looked up and said to him, "Zacchaeus, come down immediately. I must stay at your house today." 6 So he came down at once and welcomed him gladly. 7 All the people saw this and began to mutter, "He has gone to be the guest of a 'sinner.'"

8 But Zacchaeus stood up and said to the Lord, "Look, Lord! Here and now I give half of my possessions to the poor, and if I have cheated anybody out of anything, I will pay back four times the amount." 9 Jesus said to him, "Today salvation has come to this house, because this man, too, is a son of Abraham. 10 For the Son of Man came to seek and to save what was lost."

Introduction

I was expecting our lowest attendance today. We always publicize the sermon titles weeks and weeks in advance. Greed - aw, the preacher must be going to talk about money. I was expecting about 25 people.

Some years ago at the church, I did a series of classes on what the Roman Catholic Church classifies as the "Seven Deadly Sins." When I talked on the Deadly Sin of Lust, the place was packed. I was surprised that it was pretty full when I talked on gluttony. But when I got over to Greed, I think Linda was the only one there. It's just a topic we don't like to hear about.

In all my clinical experience, I've never had a person come to my clinical office and say, "I have this issue with greed I'd like for us to talk about." In 49 years I never have had that happen. It's interesting to me that only 2% of the United States population, only 2%, considers themselves upper-middle-class. Isn't that interesting? Only 2%. So we know denial is more than a river in Egypt. I think there's a lot of denial that goes on in relationship to greed.

I believe it to be operative in Zacchaeus' life. Fascinating little fella. He is Jewish. Jesus said he was. His name indicates that he was. His Jewish name, Zacchaeus, means "the Righteous One or the Just One or the One Justified." So we have a Jewish person who has become a traitor, a renegade, sinner among his own people. I have to try to set the context for you.

In Jesus' day and time his people paid what was called a 'temple tax' which involved about 8 different offerings but it was called a tax. They paid 33 1/3 percent of what they earned to the temple. They did not have a government tax or anything. The government was really the Temple. It governed almost all of their lives - every area of their life. We often talked about the people of the Old Testament paid a tithe of 10% and that we ought to do that, too. But that's just simply not true. They paid 33 1/3 percent to the Temple. Rome comes along and occupies this nation. When Rome occupied Israel, they levied a 30% government tax on the people. You get the picture? Here are these people paying 63 1/3 percent of their income to the Temple and to the occupying nation of Rome.

Tick them off? Anger them? You better believe it! Do you remember last week's message around the Zealots? That's what these people were so incited about. They were burdened. Sixty-three and one third percent of everything they earned went out of their pockets to their Church, the Temple, and to the occupying nation of Rome. So they were upset. At that point in time there were no wealthy Jews except those who had aligned themselves with Rome to collect the taxes that Rome had levied upon them.

Zacchaeus was one of those men who had become, quote, "an employee of the Roman government," to collect these 30% taxes, plus anything else they wanted to put in there upon their own people. The Scriptures tell us that he was chief of the tax collectors. Being in Jericho which was a central hub of activity was probably the best place he could have located his office. So here we have a Jew who has turned against his own people and is collecting taxes plus whatever else he wants to levy upon his own people. "A sinner," he was called. I suspect he was rejected, talked about wherever he went. Do you know any people who work for the IRS? You know they don't talk about their job at parties. They'll talk to you and when you finally ask them what they do, they'll mumble. "I need another drink. Would you like me to get you a drink?"

When's the last time you invited an IRS person over to your house for dinner? That's a legitimate job today. I guess. I know it is. Alan Blackman, I don't know if he's here or not but he's a great man. Lives in Heath Springs, works for the IRS. I remember several years ago preaching on Zacchaeus, giving him a hard time. Alan walked out. Later, Alan told me what he did. I apologized all over myself. But those people, even today are unpopular. You can only imagine how unpopular Zacchaeus was.

One cannot help or, at least I can't, raise the question, why would he do this? Why would he expose himself to that kind of rejection, hostility, name-calling, rudeness and everything else? Why would he do that? Well, you know being therapeutic, I wonder about his size and wonder if he had the Napoleon complex. I've kind of ruled that out. The truth is one little word - greed.

Greed led him to expose himself to rejection by his own people, his own community, maybe even his own family. The almighty dollar. Greed. Months and months ago there were those of us in the pulpit talking about what's really wrong with our nation is the greed. But we were the only ones saying that. Not true today. If you're reading anything today you're noticing books like the one entitled "Bailout Nation: How Greed and Easy Money Corrupted Wall Street and Shook the World Economy" by Barry Ritholtz. This guy is not religious at all. He's not coming from a religious perspective at all. Rather, he's coming from a sociological perspective, placing his finger from his perspective at the cause of all that went wrong - the unbridled greed that exists in this country today.

Timothy Keller in his book "Counterfeit Gods: The Empty Promises of Money, Sex and Power in the Only Hope That Matters," he does come from a spiritual perspective. Ernest Becker said many years ago, in his most famous book, "The Denial of Death," " God in this culture will be replaced by sex, money, and power." Friedrich Nietzsche, the German philosopher, said many years ago, "God in this culture will be replaced by money." I would remind you that Paul Tillich described what worship is. "Worship is our ultimate allegiance, our ultimate concern to whatever." The object of our ultimate concern becomes Our God, whatever that is, be it drugs, sex, money, power, doesn't matter. Whatever consumes our greatest energy then has become our God.

That was Zacchaeus' problem. That is our problem today as I see it. I have never in my lifetime seen the kind of unbridled greed that we see in our country today. Persons are making $69 million a year and are unsatisfied. What in the world is a person to do with $69 million a year? Why would anyone even want to make that kind of money? There's only one answer: Greed.

Are you aware that Jesus preached more about money and poverty than he did in any other subject - six times as much as salvation! Over and over Jesus hammers away at this thing. Why? Because it will become our ultimate concern. It will become our idol. Jesus himself said man cannot serve God and Money. When you look at that, the 'm' is capitalized. Money. Material Worth. One of those, God or money, will possess us. We cannot serve them both. (Matthew 6:24)

Again, Jesus said in Luke 15:9, "Be on your guard. Watch out, be on your guard about greed because it will consume you." It's just not the people who make $69 million a year that have issues with greed. One may not have anything and still be eaten up with greed. Greed is an attitude. It is a prevailing pattern of thought. It is something that calls forth our greatest allegiance no matter what we make. This is what had a hold of Zacchaeus' life.

One cannot help but wonder, being one of the wealthiest men in Jericho and Israel with all this money to buy whatever he chose to buy, Zacchaeus was not happy. Why?

About two decades ago in America there started a movement to study 'happiness.' I was fascinated by the beginning of those studies because I really don't know what happiness is. I know what health is. That's what I deal with and I know one cannot be happy without being healthy. I can help a person create health. I wondered how these people were going to establish sensible research to determine happiness. But they did. They came up with some fascinating happiness surveys and scales. One of the interesting things they found was that money itself makes a contribution to one's happiness. Money will make a contribution to our happiness, and overall well-being to a point. That point is when our physical needs are met, when our housing, food, clothing, all these things, all these needs that are normally natural, when they are met and our money is making a contribution to meeting those needs, money will increase our happiness. But, there is a point of diminishing returns. When all of those needs are met happiness cannot be purchased with money.

A boat was going up the lake, some lake, one day and had a crowd on it. There happened to be a therapist on it and they came by a $3 million dollar house, two Mercedes sitting in the back yard, two boats at the dock, one on the lift and one on the water. Two people sitting up there on the front porch in the shade and someone on the boat said, "Goll-lee! Don't you know they're so happy they can hardly stand it?" The therapist could not say a word because he's been seeing them in therapy for over a year.

Money reaches a point where it does not contribute to our happiness. When our essential needs are met, when we have a little extra change in the pocket, when we can put a little jelly on the bread, then what money does for us starts diminishing.

I project that's what happened to Zacchaeus. This deep greed so filled his heart it led him to turn his back on his own people, collect money from his own people and for a time, for the season, he was as happy as happy could be. But then it went south. Loneliness, feelings of rejection, scorn. How much are they worth? We find him seeking someone he has apparently heard about. As he tries to make his way to Jesus on the road to Jericho, I can just imagine that crowd, every chance they got there would be an elbow in the ribs. I can only imagine how they push this fellow around and scorned him in that crowded community.

Zacchaeus runs up the road and climbs up a tree. Why? Why would he act like a child, disrespectful and dishonoring? He's already the recipient of all kinds of scorn. Why would he? Something deep within him is eating him up. Something that greed and all the money he's acquired has not filled. He's seeking to see Jesus.

Andrew Carnegie made his millions in steel. At the age of 33 he wrote these words. Keep in mind, here's a man who built and paid for 2059 libraries throughout the country. Very, very unselfish in his latter years. At age 33, this is what he wrote. "Man must have an idol." For a non-Theologian, that's a pretty interesting statement. *"Man must have an idol. The amassing of wealth is one of the worst species of idolatry. No idol is more debasing than the worship of money. Whatever I engage in, I must push inordinately, therefore, should I be careful to choose the life which will be the most elevating in character. To continue much longer, overwhelmed by business cares with most of my thoughts wholly upon the way to make money in the shortest time, will degrade me beyond hope of permanent recovery. I will resign my business at age 35."* [33] Wow! What insight. His self understanding was that he was so pursuant of wealth at all costs that he had to change.

Zacchaeus came to that place. Something has got to change. I am so wounded by greed my life is out of focus. My life is being consumed. So Zacchaeus acts like a child and runs ahead, gets up into that tree. To his amazement, Jesus comes by and looks up and calls his name. You know he knows your name. Jesus says, "Zacchaeus, come down. Today I'm going to have a meal in your house." And the crowd is appalled that this so-called religious teacher would stoop so low as to go to the sinner's house and eat with him. They were astounded.

Zacchaeus comes down out of a tree. Notice immediately what he says. Here is a man wounded by greed that has just been healed. Notice what he says. I know he's been healed because anytime Jesus touches your heart and you allow his finger to run around to your hip where you carry that wallet, you've been healed. I guarantee it. The song says 'somebody touched me.' Well, we are talking about touching hearts; we're not talking about touching pocketbooks. We don't even like that kind of language.

Zacchaeus comes out of the tree and he said to Jesus, "Half of my wealth, I'll give to the poor." Wow! You talk about touched! Half of everything I have, Jesus, I'm going to designate, donate, give to the poor. Then he takes another step and he says, "If I have wronged anyone..." He knows good and well he has. Rather than being biblically legal as

[33] Keller, Timothy. Counterfeit Gods: The Empty Promises of Money, Sex and Power, and The Only Hope that Matters. New York: Apple Books 2009. p 68

Leviticus 5:16 says and give them 20% interest for the wrong, Zacchaeus says, "I will give 80 percent to those I have wronged." Eighty percent! Wow! What a healing. What a healing that has taken place.

God would desire that same kind of healing for you. It is not anything wrong with money. That's not it. It is the love of money. It is what the scripture says in 1 Timothy 6:18. It is the love of money that becomes the root of all evil, not money itself. Money is simply a tool. That's all. Just a tool.

I was amazed a few years ago when the Presbyterian Church came out in one of their Assembly meetings and said we are asking all Presbyterians to give up their guns. I thought, "Yeah, and when they pry these cold dead fingers away from my gun, they can take it." Guns aren't the problem. Money is not the problem. It's simply a tool that we allow to consume us.

Conclusion

I have never believed in tithing during my entire Christian experience because I found out early in my reading of the Scriptures, that was just incorrect. I am not responsible to God for 10% of what I have. I am responsible to God for 100% of what I have. How I earn it, how I spend it, and how I give it to benevolent causes. They don't have anything to do with 10%. When I came to that realization, there was a release and a freedom within me in relationship to material things. They are not mine. Everything I have is on loan. I'm asked to be a steward of that which has been loaned to me. It is also true of you. Don't think it's only the billionaires and millionaires in Washington and New York that are greedy. No. We got greed right here among us. Trust me. Greed's right here.

I would pray for your healing, that you would come to the realization that all this is a tool that God has placed in your hands to be used for your needs and God's glory. May we, like Zacchaeus, be healed today.

Let us pray.

Oh Lord, thank you for this marvelous story. A story of a man whose heart is significantly touched and whose life is radically altered. All of us are wounded by many different things. Help us to believe because of Zacchaeus' story, that our wounds can be healed when we seek and allow you to find us. By your stripes we are healed. May we experience the truth of that. In Jesus' name. Amen.

May God bless you and keep you healing.

WHAT HAPPENS TO US IS NOT THAT IMPORTANT.

IT IS WHAT HAPPENS TO WHAT HAPPENS TO US THAT IS IMPORTANT.

Harold S. Kushner, born April 3, 1935, was a young rabbi serving a local congregation in Boston when he was wounded. His two year old son Aaron was diagnosed with "progeria," or rapid aging disease and would die in his early teens. The family lived with this wound until Aaron died two days before his fourteenth birthday and then the pain became a different type of wound. Yet, Rabbi Kushner wrote a touching heart-warming book that has helped to heal millions of people wounded by the tragedy of loss.

Kushner, Harold S. <u>When Bad Things Happen to Good People</u>. New Your: Avon Books. 1981

CHAPTER 14

DIVES: WOUNDED BY GREED AND NOT HEALED

Text: Luke 16:19-31

CIT: *(Central Idea of the text)*
            Dives was wounded by greed unwilling to use any of his
            wealth to heal the pain of others.

Thesis: Let us seek healing from our wounds of Greed while there
            is still time.

Purpose:

- Major Objective: Evangelistic
- Specific Objective: Through the power of the Holy Spirit,
  I hope to lead each of us into healing and becoming healers.

Introduction

Outline:
   I.   Wounded By Greed - v.19
   II. Wounded Presented - vs.20-22
   III. Wounded Rejected - v.23
   IV. Wounds Can Carry You To Hell - vs.24-26
   V.   Wounded Healer Want-To-Be - vs.27-31

Conclusion:

"...wealth
in and of itself
is not a vice.
Poverty
in and of itself
is not a virtue."

The Word of the Lord

Luke 16:19–31

19 "There was a rich man who was dressed in purple and fine linen and lived in luxury every day. 20 At his gate was laid a beggar named Lazarus, covered with sores 21 and longing to eat what fell from the rich man's table. Even the dogs came and licked his sores.

22 "The time came when the beggar died and the angels carried him to Abraham's side. The rich man also died and was buried. 23 In hell, where he was in torment, he looked up and saw Abraham far away, with Lazarus by his side. 24 So he called to him, 'Father Abraham, have pity on me and send Lazarus to dip the tip of his finger in water and cool my tongue because I'm in agony in this fire.'

25 "But Abraham replied, 'Son, remember that in your lifetime you received your good things, while Lazarus received bad things, but now he is comforted here and you are in agony. 26 And besides all this, between us and you a great chasm has been fixed, so that those who want to go from here to you cannot, nor can anyone crossover from there to us.'

27 "He answered, 'Then I beg you, father, send Lazarus to my father's house, 28 for I have five brothers. Let him warn them, so that they will not also come to this place of torment.'

29 "Abraham replied, 'They have Moses and the Prophets; let them listen to them.'

30" 'No, Father Abraham,' he said, 'but if someone from the dead goes to them they will repent.'

31 "He said to him, 'If they do not listen to Moses and the Prophets, they will not be convinced even if someone rises from the dead.'"

Introduction

A Frenchman named Anaatole France made this statement in reference to America: "In every well-governed state wealth is a sacred thing. In democracies it is the only sacred thing." Well, I pray that's not true. I do not believe that to be true. I understand that perspective; I just don't believe it be totally true.

George Bernard Shaw wrote, "We have no more right to consume happiness without producing it than we have the right to consume wealth without producing it." I believe that fully. For those who know me well enough to jump all over me and critique me, often call me a bleeding heart liberal who wants to take from the rich and give to the poor. Well, I do not believe that at all. I believe what George Bernard Shaw said, that we do not have the right to consume wealth when we are not producing it. But, as there are Lazarus's in the Bible and in this story, there are Lazarus's in our world today. For those of us who are able and capable, Jesus gave us a mandate to take care of those Lazarus's of our day.

Jesus spent more time, more words, more parables about wealth and the poor than he did with anything else. But let me assure you of something, several things about this parable – and it is a parable. It was not a true story in that it was not an historical story. There are those who want to make it so because Lazarus is named. But, it's in a string of parables that Jesus is giving, so why would he change? So it's a parable. It's interesting that Lazarus, the poor beggar, is named and the rich man is not. I've called him Dives because that's the Latin word for rich. In theological circles he has come to be known as Dives, the rich man and Lazarus. I think it's noteworthy that Jesus names the poor beggar and the rich person is left unnamed. I find that significant.

Let me assure us that wealth in and of itself is not a vice. Poverty in and of itself is not a virtue. There's nothing virtuous about just being poor. Nothing evil about being wealthy. It is what we allow these two to do to us. Poverty, which I will speak on next week, can be just as wounding as wealth as can be.

We have this tragic Parable before us of how one is wounded by greed. And I would like to call to your memory last week of Zacchaeus who had traded his life for a life of wealth, having turned his back own his own country and his own countrymen earning the wealth that he earned. But Zacchaeus was healed! Jesus spoke to him and Zacchaeus immediately gave half of his wealth to the poor and then said for those that I've taken illegally from I'll give it back 80%, not 20% like the Bible says. I'll give 80%.

So, we see one who was wounded by greed, whose life had been greatly wounded by greed, but one who is healed. In his healing and out of his healing, he becomes a wounded healer. That is possible for all of us, no matter what our wound.

But in Dives' case he is not healed. One who lives by wearing purple (the Scriptures give us the picture of a lavish lifestyle), Dives has a lavish lifestyle and there's no vice in that. But there is a beggar outside his door who he discounts, walks by, and fails to give any kind of care, compassionate concern at all. They both die. This is not a parable about eternity. Theology about eternity should not be built on this parable. I've read those commentators who say we know why Lazarus was saved quote, "Because he believed in Jesus and Dives did not." But, that's not in the parable at all. That's not what the parable's about. The parable is about the misuse of wealth that's simple and clear. The misuse of the goodnesses, the Graces, mercies that God has entrusted. It does not mean we have to do what Zacchaeus did and give half of our wealth to the poor. It didn't mean that. It doesn't mean what Jesus said to the rich young ruler. He said, "Give away everything that you have and follow me." (Matthew 19:21) We don't have to do that, but what we do have to do to be followers of Our Lord is to not be so wounded by greed that we do not see those in and around us who are the Lazarus's of our world.

In those days they did not have fine linen and napkins like we have today to wipe their hands on. They would normally take crust, pieces of bread and wipe their hands to get the meal grease and oils off their hands. Then the bread would just go to the floor and it would then be discarded outside. The wild dogs and other animals would eat it. Dives did not even privilege Lazarus with crumbs from his table. We know that Dives knew Lazarus, had seen him. How do we know that? Well, in Hell, he sees Father Abraham and he sees Lazarus whom he recognizes and calls by name when he said, "Father Abraham, send Lazarus. Let him dip the tip of his finger in the water to cool my tormented tongue." So he knew he was outside his gate. He knew he was in the condition that he was in. He knew that. He saw the pain and the suffering of those around him and willfully chose to do nothing. Willfully chose to do nothing.

In Hell Dives sees Father Abraham. One of the things Jesus did with his parable was to confront them very clearly. Just because you are a child of Abraham, your Eternal faith is not settled. Just because we were raised in some fashion in a Christian church; just because our name's on some church form somewhere, that's not what counts. It is what we do. Do we need personal faith? Of course. I'm not denying that. But over and over again Jesus talks about walking the walk and part of the walk is taking care of those in and around us who are unable, not unwilling, to care adequately for themselves. It becomes imperative that we as followers of the Compassionate One, see these as persons in need of our compassion.

We are moving into our 27th year together. It was 26 years this past May. How is it that we've been together that long? Well you know I'm just a wonderful person and you're just a wonderful group of people but I don't think that's it. Here's what I think it is. I think we have been able to be together and to stay focused outside of ourselves. That's where churches get in trouble. They get divided about what color lawn mower to buy, what color carpet, etc. We don't deal with those things. If we need a lawn mower we let a committee do that. If we need new carpet, we get a committee to do that. We don't deal with that stuff. What we deal with are the needs of those around us, the Lazarus's among us. We stay focused. They have said to me from the Presbytery several years ago, "Gene, you really need to think about what giving that lakeside money to the Presbyterian Church would mean to you and your church from a reputation standpoint." I said, "I don't care about the reputation." But overall last year we gave 35% of our budget. The year before was 37% of our budget. 100% of what is collected here at the lake goes to the needs of those folks in and around us who are the Lazarus's of our world. That's why we've been able to stay together all these years. We are focused on those outside of ourselves who need us, who need a portion of our monies, who need our compassionate presence, who need our prayers, our visits, our concern. We keep our eyes off ourselves!

I take great pride in you for being that kind of people. I don't think we could have been together all these years if we didn't have the same mind and the same heart about caring for the "least of these" (Matthew 25:40) in and around us. We put untold amount of energy and money into the prison system to rehabilitate the inmates to train others. One of our students, Eddie Woods, just took a church in Edgefield. Linda and I went down and I preached his installation service. He is one of our many disciples that has learned well. About 4 to 5 young Blacks in Edgefield, early every Sunday morning are playing basketball about two blocks from his church. What does he do? Did he go down there and jump on them for not being in church? No. He learned from us. He went down there and said, "I have ice boxes filled with ice cold Gatorade. If you will give me 5 minutes I'll give everybody here a bottle of Gatorade." That was his first time. He goes every week. Have they come to the church yet? No. They've started calling him the Gatorade Man. He and his people are doing the same thing in the town. 'What can we do for you? What are your needs? Where are your Lazarus's? That is what we are proud of. That is what has held us together. That will keep us from being wounded by greed. When we share out of what we have, we will not be wounded beyond healing as Dives was. If we're wounded, we can be healed as Zacchaeus was. But it is in the sharing with the "least of these" that we are healed.

I was reminded of Jesus's words to the church at Laodicea in the third chapter of Revelation. This is what he is saying. "I know your deeds. You are neither cold nor hot. I wish you were either one or the other! So, because you are lukewarm, neither hot nor cold, I will spew you out of my mouth." (I believe that means to vomit.) "You say, 'I am rich, I have acquired wealth, and do not need a thing.' But you do not realize you are wretched, pitiful, poor, naked and blind." (Rev. 3: 14-17) Wow! You think you're something but you're not.

Conclusion

In Texas many years ago I read in the history of a little west Texas town about a church who had a pretty good plot of property. Lo and behold, with some research, they found they had oil on their property. Before the first oil well was dug, they closed membership to that congregation. And it was a gusher. But I don't think I need to tell you that today the church does not exist. That's what happens when we think we're rich. That's what happens when we close membership on our wealth and will not share it with the Lazarus's of our world.

Let us pray.

Oh Lord, thank you for this tragic story. We could wish that like Zacchaeus, Dives' eyes could have been opened and he could have seen, but he saw too late. Help us to know that any of our wounds can carry us to eternal separation from you but especially the wound of greed. Help us as a people of faith to be open-handed and compassionate to all of those in our part of the world. May it be so. In Jesus' name. Amen.

May God bless you and keep you being healed.

WHAT HAPPENS TO US IS NOT THAT IMPORTANT.

**IT IS WHAT HAPPENS TO WHAT HAPPENS
TO US THAT IS IMPORTANT.**

The Buddhist Christine Longaker has said, "What makes us feel hopeless is not our difficult situation; it's being isolated in our suffering, fear or grief, and not being able to connect with others. When we meet each other in relationships without dominance, without armor, in equal measures of humility and assertiveness, we connect with others and they connect with us. In that connection we experience congruence, empathy, and unconditional positive regard, sharing wounds, sharing strengths, sharing healing."

Longaker, C. (1997). <u>Facing Death And Finding Hope.</u> New York: Doubleday.

CHAPTER 15

LAZARUS: WOUNDED BY POVERTY

Text: Luke 16:19-25

CIT: *(Central Idea of the text)*
             Lazarus, poor ulcerated beggar, died and was carried by
             angels to the heavenly banquet.

Thesis: Although some wounds are not healed while on this earth
             they will be.

Purpose:

- Major Objective: Doctrinal
- Specific Objective: Through the power of the Holy Spirit,
  I hope to increase our awareness and prayer for those
  wounded by poverty.

Introduction

Outline:
   I.   Wounded By Poverty - vs.20-21
   II.   Wounded Until Death - v.22
   III. Healed In Heaven - vs.22, 25

Conclusion

"...consider,
not just prayerfully consider,
behaviorally consider
the orphans
and the widows..."

"I am convinced
that in order
to deal with terrorism,
to deal with our own
crime rate,
we must deal with
the issue of poverty
because it is the seedbed
that breeds the
us-against-them thinking,
the pack, mob mentality
in this deep-seated belief
of being less than."

"No matter how bad this life becomes,
no matter how gory
the wounds we receive,
there will be a better day."

The Word of the Lord

Luke 16:19-25

19 "There was a rich man who was dressed in purple and fine linen and lived in luxury every day. 20 At his gate was laid a beggar named Lazarus, covered with sores 21 and longing to eat what fell from the rich man's table. Even the dogs came and licked his sores.

22 "The time came when the beggar died and the angels carried him to Abraham's side. The rich man also died and was buried. 23 In hell, where he was in torment, he looked up and saw Abraham far away, with Lazarus by his side. 24 So he called to him, 'Father Abraham, have pity on me and send Lazarus to dip the tip of his finger in water and cool my tongue because I'm in agony in this fire.'

25 "But Abraham replied, 'Son, remember that in your lifetime you received your good things, while Lazarus received bad things, but now he is comforted here and you are in agony.

Introduction

I recently read a story of a family who almost perished by starvation. They lived on the second floor of a building. On the first floor of the same building was a church. There's just something wrong with that picture. My criticism of the contemporary church of today is that we have profession without practice, a talk without walk, a creed without deed, and a belief without behavior. I believe in many ways we stand condemned just as that church, in my thinking, stands condemned.

This morning we consider the wound of poverty. I want to reassure you as I shared with some of you that were here last week, and I reassure you today that although accused of it at times, I am not a bleeding heart liberal who believes that we should take from the rich and give to the poor. I do not believe that.

George Bernard Shaw said, "We do not have the right to happiness if we're not producing it, nor do we have the right to wealth if we are not producing it." But we must consider that there are Lazarus's among us who are unable to produce wealth. I have little to no tolerance for those who are able to work and will not. I have to watch my prejudice there. 2 Thessalonians 3:10 says, "He that will not work must not eat." Proverbs 6:6 says, "Sluggard, go to the ant and observe her ways and become wise." I really believe scripture has little tolerance for those who are able to work and will not, and nor do I. But I reiterate there are those Lazarus's among us who are unable to produce. And in the scriptures that category of resident in poverty were characterized by two groups of people, the widow and the orphan.

Fifty-nine times in the Old Testament and twenty-six times in the New Testament these two symbols of poverty are referred to. A total of eighty-five times. That's a pretty heavy thing. I will only read two versus, one from the Old Testament and one from the New that lift out for us the need of these two categories of people who represent poverty in that day.

Exodus 22:22. "Do not take advantage of a widow or an orphan. If you do they will cry out to me. I will certainly hear their cry. My anger will be aroused and I will kill you with a sword. Your wives will become widows and your children fatherless." Wow! That's pretty harsh. The scripture is saying, here's two groups of people who are living in poverty and you will not abuse them, you will not take advantage of them, and if you do, quid pro quo.

The New Testament text is James 1:27. "Religion that God our Father accepts as pure and faultless is this: to look after the orphans and widows in their distress and to keep oneself from being polluted by the world." Wow! Is that not pretty clear? A religion, a belief system, a faith that God accepts as pure and faultless is this: consider, not just prayerfully consider, behaviorally consider the orphans and the widows, the symbols of those in poverty in your community and in your world.

At times I become sick and tired, at other times just embarrassed, at the beliefism that exists in our culture. You just believe in Jesus and everything is wonderful, grand and glorious. I really don't think the scriptures portray followers of Christ in that light. I believe the scriptures portray us as persons who are to be concerned and compassionate.

Who are the poverty-ridden in our culture? In my research it's a little bit hard to determine, but finally I concluded through the latest 2010 census that in America, poverty is defined this way:

1. If you are a family of five and you make less than $26,338 annually, you are living in poverty.
2. 39.1 million people in America live in poverty.
3. 15.9% of the residents in South Carolina live in poverty according to that definition.
4. 7.1 million children in poverty in America have no health insurance. [34]

Poverty worldwide is much more drastic than the way I've just defined it in America. Gandhi made the statement about poverty like this. "Poverty is the worst form of violence." Aristotle said many, many years ago that, "The mother of revolution and crime is poverty." The mother of revolution and crime. Ben Franklin in his unique way of expression put it like this. "Poverty deprives a man of spirit and virtue. It is hard for an empty bag to stand upright."

The wounds of poverty. Would you consider for a moment the life of Lazarus, one who is in poverty so deeply that he is enabled by someone, i.e., brought to a wealthy person's gate and left with his tin cup to beg for coins. Can you consider in that benign statement of scripture that Abraham says to Dives that in Lazarus's life, he received bad things? Can you stay with me for a moment while we examine the wounds of poverty?

Wayne Oates, a professor, was formerly at The Medical School of Kentucky and later was a professor at Southern Baptist Seminary in Louisville. He was born in Greenville, South Carolina on a Mill Hill, finished high school at Parker where my wife finished. He graduated several decades before she did. In 1968 he wrote a little book at age 65 entitled "The Struggle to Be Free." The freedom that he speaks of in that little book which became a classic is the struggle with the dynamics of poverty, the wounds of poverty and what that creates. He listed and expounds upon them as three. I find them so very clearly evident today.

The first wound of poverty is that concept of us against them, that

---

[34] The Center for American Progress

concept of separateness, of being separated from. Unlike. Against. Us and Them. And that dynamic produces the wound of what he called 'pack thinking.' Mob mentality. I submit to you, gangs. But in the context of this deep-seated belief of us and them, they have it - we don't - creates a bond, a pack, mob thinking and mentality. [35]

The latest book that I've read entitled "<u>The Making of a Terrorist</u>" by James J. F. Forest spends many pages with this concept of poverty and how that concept produces these three: (1) us against them, (2) pack mentality, and then Oates spends the rest of his book talking about (3) this deep-seated sense of inferiority. Poor self-worth. And how after degree after degree, acclaim after acclaim, at age 65 he is still struggling to be free from this deep sense of being less than. This deep feeling of not measuring up, of not being as good as. Poverty produces that wound and it is a wound to the very core. I am convinced that in order to deal with terrorism, to deal with our own crime rate, we must deal with the issue of poverty because it is the seedbed that breeds the us-against-them thinking, the pack, mob mentality in this deep-seated belief of being less than.

I could, as many of you know who have been around me for a while, personally illustrate in detail some of the injury of poverty but I will not bore you with that today, only to illustrate with this one point. I think two years ago it was National Secretaries Day. I took our office manager to lunch and at lunch we were talking about how to improve our work situation and do various things in our work. She says to me, "May I get a little personal?" And I said, "Well of course." She said, "I'm aware of the hours that you put in and I know that you're aware of the hours that you put in because you logged them. I'm just wondering why you do that." I said to her almost tongue and cheek but with a significant element of truth, "I feel so absolutely worthless that I strive to redeem myself through work." And without missing a beat, she said, "I thought you told me you had spent years in therapy." Well, there's some things therapy doesn't help. It is so primal within that wound of poverty, so deep, this sense of 'I am not as good as - I am not as worthy as,' that one will go to all kinds of lengths in one's life to address that

[35] Oates, Wayne E. The Struggle to Be Free. Philadelphia, Te Westminster Press, 1983

deep-seated need. Some of them are more socially acceptable like work and others are less socially acceptable. But that deep longing, that deep belief is there.

The wounds of poverty are far-reaching and Lazarus was not healed from that one. There are wounds in our lives that will not be healed in our lifetime. We will take them with us to meet the Lord. But there are some things we can do about wounds, even this one, whether they are healed completely or not.

Years ago after Linda and I married she asked me, "Are you happy?" And, gentlemen, don't ever answer that question this way. I said, "I am as happy as I <u>can</u> be." Well, we spent months working that statement out, so I strongly encourage you to be smarter than that. But there was an experience that helped her to understand what I was saying. We were out on the deck one Friday evening. It was a magnificent sunset. We had a fine filet mignon cooked just right. Bleeding. And for us, an expensive bottle of wine. It was not our usual Morgan David or Thunderbird. Everything had just gone perfect. She said to me, "You look depressed. What's wrong?" I said, "I feel guilty," and of course that strikes a note, too, men. Don't use that word either. You start conjuring up all kinds of images in one's head. So I hurriedly said, "You know we've had this magnificently beautiful meal. Two-thirds of the world's population may have gotten a bowl of rice today if they were lucky." And, I said, "The only thing that keeps me from having to choke this meal down is to know that we are contributing and doing everything we can to touch the wounds of poverty. That was Dives mistake. Nothing wrong with him eating lavishly, wearing purple and fine linens. Nothing wrong with that at all. But the Word tells us he ignored the wounds of the man lying at his gate. We must not in the name of the follower of Christ ignore the wounds of poverty and live as we do.

Conclusion

Abraham says to Dives as Lazarus is by his side, "In life this man received bad things, but now he is comforted." That's part of our story. No matter how bad this life becomes, no matter how gory the wounds we receive, there will be a better day. And it was that belief which kept the persons of slavery and the persons in deep poverty in that part of our history, hopeful and living. They expressed that magnificent belief in the Hereafter through songs about Heaven. A line or two in that Black spiritual talks about 'all of God's chillun got shoes' when many of them didn't have shoes on earth. And, 'we goin' walk all over God's heaven.' Those Black spirituals like the gospel train, "Swing Low Sweet Chariot," kept them alive and hopeful until things changed. For many it did not change until they got off that gospel train. But for us as Christ's Community we are called to do all we can for the wounded, no matter what their wounds are and in doing so many of our own wounds are healed as we become wounded healers to those in and around us.

Let us pray.

O Lord, for this beautiful story, tragic as it is, we give you thanks for the hope-filled ending of Lazarus's life. A life of poverty, wounds and disease but an eternity of comfort and bliss. Instill deep within us two things: a commitment to be compassionate with all those who are wounded and a commitment to our faith that one day life as we know it will be over and we will experience the fullness of our spirituality. In Jesus' name. Amen.

God bless you and keep you hopeful.

WHAT HAPPENS TO US IS NOT THAT IMPORTANT.

IT IS WHAT HAPPENS TO WHAT HAPPENS TO US THAT IS IMPORTANT.

Carl Gustav Jung (July 26, 1875 – June 6, 1961) was wounded for 17 years (1913-1930) with what was called "a confrontation with the unconscious – a creative illness or menaced by a psychosis." Whatever it was it was a "dark night of the soul." Yet, he became the founder of analytical psychology which has been a healer of millions of people the world over.

Shamdasani, Sonu, Edited. The Red Book Liber Novus. New York: WW Norton & Company

CHAPTER 16

PAUL: A WOUNDED HEALER

Text: 2 Corinthians 12:7-10

CIT: *(Central Idea of the text)*
              Paul had a wound that was continuous, resulting in his
              increased humility.

Thesis: We can become a wounded healer even when the wound
              is continuous.

Purpose:
              • Major Objective: Supportive
              • Specific Objective: Through the power of the Holy Spirit,
                I hope to lead each of us in becoming wounded healers.

Introduction

Outline:
      I.   The Vexation Of The Wound - vs.7; Galatians 4:15, 6:11
            1. Wounded By Satan? - v.7
            2. Wounded By God? - vs.8-9
      II.   The Victory Over The Wound - vs.9-10
            1. Paul's Request - v.8
            2. God's Refusal - v.9
            3. Paul's Realization - v.10

Conclusion

"If it just wasn't for this wound,
if I didn't have this wound,
I'd be doing some grand, glorious and
wonderful thing for Jesus.
The wound,
the thorn,
is an excuse."

"It is in the presence
of our woundedness,
we are at our best."

The Word of the Lord

Before our text, 2 Corinthians 12:7-10, Paul has shared some of the great revelations that he has experienced. We think some of those came about, at least one or maybe two, from his near-death experiences. As he shares these wonderful revelations that he's experienced he then launches into this passage. He says in order for me to not be conceited over those marvelous spiritual experiences, he had this thorn in the flesh. I am going to use wounded instead of thorn in my reading, so if you would pay attention carefully as you follow along with me. I do not want to do injustice to the scripture but I believe that it fits.

2 Corinthians 12:7-10

7 To keep me from becoming conceited because of these surpassingly great revelations, there was given to me a thorn (wound) in my flesh, a messenger (wound) of Satan to torment me. 8 Three times I pleaded with the Lord to take it (the wound) away from me. 9 But he said to me, "My grace is sufficient for you, for my power is made perfect in weakness (woundedness)." Therefore, I will boast all the more gladly about my weaknesses (woundedness) so that Christ's power may rest on me. That is why, for Christ's sake, I delight in weaknesses (woundedness), and insults, in hardships, in persecutions, in difficulties. For when I am weak (wounded), then I am strong.

Introduction

Let me call your attention also to that printed piece preceding the 10th chapter written by Alastair V. Campbell. "The authority with which we offer help to others derives from our acquaintance with grief.... The wounded healer heals, because he or she is able to convey, as much by presence as by word used, both an awareness and a transcendence of loss... Wounded healers heal because they, to some degree at least, have entered the depths of their own experience of loss and in those depths found hope again." [36]

Let me introduce you, if you have not met her as of yet, to Willa of

---

[36] Campbell, Alastair V. Rediscovering Pastoral Care. Philadelphia: Westminster John Knox Press. 1981, p 51.

Wateree. She is an 18 month old yellow Lab that belongs to the Rollins family. Did you hear that voice from the wilderness cry that she belongs to the neighborhood. Willa, unlike most dogs, does not wag her tail. She wags her entire body. And she roams this neighborhood. Everyone within a mile or two of here has a Willa story. She visits this one home and when she gets tired of playing with their dog Emma, she goes and sits in the golf cart and waits till they take her home.

One family brings her home in the front seat of a Mercedes. The calls I receive always start like this, "Reverend Rollins, we have your dog. She is sweet. She is so, so precious." I want to say to them, "Beat her. Rock her. Scold her. Send her home." But, of course I don't say that. Willa is the socialite that she is because she has never been wounded. Her world is safe, happy and predictable. So, therefore, she does not have any qualms at all about entering into it. And she goes through the neighborhood wagging her body like a barroom dancer, tantalizing everyone and making everyone think how precious and sweet she is. She's never been wounded.

We have an older dog, Wateree Will, 2. We call him Ree. He's almost 11, who never leaves our yard, ever, unless he's walking with us. We can be gone overnight, put him out food. He will not leave that yard because he's been wounded. His world out there is not safe, it is not secure, it is not predictable. It is not necessarily a happy place so he stays at home. When he was six months of age, I put him in dog school training where he was physically abused. At a year's age, he was bitten by a huge Copperhead in the face and had a traumatic 3-day recovery. When he was about two and a half, he was hit by a car on Highway 97 trying to get to the other side where I was. When he was about four he was struck by lightning - lit up like a Christmas tree. When he was about 5, he developed a knee problem and had to have surgery with a steel plate put in his knee. He contracted MRSA as a result of that and had to get shots daily for 21 days. His world is not safe. He is wounded.

I believe these two represent very clearly two types of people in our world. There are those folks who are basically unwounded to any traumatic degree. You've heard me say all summer, we're all wounded and we are to a degree. But there are those people who were born into very functional families. Their grandparents were functional and loved them. Their parents were functional and loved them. They were in good neighborhoods, secure, happy worlds. They were in good schools, receive good high school educations and went off the Ivy League colleges. They received a wonderful education preparing them for very fruitful vocations. They acquired those fruitful vocations and along the way married a good functional spouse and they produced healthy functional children. There are those people like that. Some of my colleagues argue with me and say, "No they're not. They are just in denial." I want to say, "No. No, it's my life experience that I find folks who just had it well, and that's good. I think that's wonderful. Not my story but it's wonderful."

There are the Willa's of the world and then there are the Ree's who have been battered and beaten by chance, circumstance, ill-health, abuse and a lot of other wounds in life. They retreat and they stay pretty well to themselves in their own homes and families where it is pretty much safe. They do not venture far.

Then I believe there are some other kinds of folks that are represented by Paul. Paul was wounded. Yet, he was a preacher, a missionary, a traveler out into his world receiving some other wounds along the way. But in his woundedness, he would not be restricted. He would not be isolated. We do not know what Paul's wound was. He called it a thorn. In the Greek the word is skolops which is a stake sharpened on one end that they might drive in the ground for a tent peg. Paul is using that word traumatically. There is in my life this skolops, this stake that has been driven into me.

There are those Abundant Life people, "healers," who say if we are not healed from the wounds of our life then our faith is the reason. We simply do not have faith enough. If we had faith enough, God in Christ Our Healer, would heal us. Well, to those people I challenge to show me a life any more faithful than the Apostle Paul. Show it to me. I want to see it. Observe it. I do not see his lack of faith in any realm.

Among the same people there are those who say, "Well he had unconfessed sin. If you have faith and your sin is confessed up-to-date, God will heal you. If you're not healed, it's because of one of those two reasons." Paul was a sinner. He says, "I am the chief of sinners," (1 Timothy 1:15) but I cannot see anywhere in this scripture that indicates at all that Paul had unconfessed sin in his life that may have prevented him from being healed. Paul was simply not healed.

There are those among us who will not be healed by God in Christ, by physicians, surgeries, medicines, or anything else. We will not be healed. We will carry that wound to our death. It's our choice as to how we are going to live.

Paul said, "I prayed and prayed and prayed." Don't be fooled by that three times. That's the Trinity. Paul prayed and prayed and prayed that God would take this skolops, this thorn from his life. Paul believed that he could be a better preacher, that he could be a better missionary, that he could be a better witness, that he could be a better person if this thorn were out of his life. The thorn, we don't know what it was. There is indication in Galatians that it could have been his poor eyesight. He says to the Galatian people who loved him dearly, "…if you would have taken out your own eyes and given them to me." (Galatians 4:15) It indicates he had eye problems.

In 2 Corinthians 10:10, it talks about his unimpressive stature. Some believe that it was the little Napoleon stature, weaken structure and unimpressive, that was his thorn. There are others who believe that it was more of a spiritual thing in that he held the clothes of Stephen, the first Deacon, and gave consent to those who stoned him to death. (Acts 8:1) Paul carried this guilt to his grave. There are others who jokingly say, "Well, it had to be his wife." Paul was married at one point in time. He had to be to be a member of the Sanhedrin. He was either widowed or divorced. One of the two, because at the time of the writing there was no indication - in fact just the opposite - he indicates he is single.

I personally believe that Paul's thorn was the malaria that he lived with. We have indications, several passages that speak about him in ways that would fit well with uncured malaria. It was rampant in those times. But whatever Paul's thorn was, earlier there was a part of him who believed he could be a better person if he were not wounded, wounded by this thorn in the flesh, whatever it was. So, he prayed God would remove it and God would not. There is nothing incongruent with son-ship and thorn-ship. Nothing incompatible with those two.

Nothing incongruent. Because you're wounded doesn't say anything about your spirituality or the lack thereof. Wounded is wounded.

I want us to take a look at this man who in spite of his wounds believed that he could be of ministry, of healing, of health to others. Now, there are those who are wounded and because of their thorn, wound, they will take the position, an 'excuse-it' position. If I did not have this wound, I would be this marvelous servant of God. If it just wasn't for this wound, if I didn't have this wound, I'd be doing some grand, glorious and wonderful thing for Jesus. The wound, the thorn, is an excuse.

God confronted a man in the desert of Midian, through a burning bush and he said to Moses, "I want you to go down and deliver my people in Egypt from their slavery. I've heard their cries and they're not suffering any longer. I want them delivered by your hand." Moses said, "Who am I? I'm a shepherd out here in the middle of nowhere. In fact, a fugitive from Egypt. I killed an Egyptian. Who am I?" And God said to Moses, "Don't worry about that. I'll be with you." And then Moses says, (go to Exodus 3 and 4 and read it). Moses said, "Who are you? I don't know your name." And God says, "I am that I am," meaning I will be whatever it is I want to be. And then Moses says to him, "They won't believe me. Why are they going to believe me?" And God says, "Moses, what is that you have in your hand?" And he said, "A stick, staff." "Throw it on the ground." He threw it on the ground and it became a pit viper. A little test of faith. Moses picked it up and it became a staff again. God said to Moses, "You'll do all kind of miraculous things. They'll believe you." Then Moses said, "You need someone who can speak well. I just can't speak. I am not an eloquent speaker." And God, almost exasperated at this time, says, "All right. Take your brother Aaron with you. He's a great speaker. I'll be with both of you." And then Moses said, "Nah. Just send someone else. I'm too wounded. I'm just too wounded. No one knows me. They won't believe me when I tell them I know you. They won't even believe who you are. I'm just so wounded. I'm not going to be good." But, he does change his mind.

There's a lot of those who never change their mind. 'I'm just so wounded, so impaired, that God is not going to be able to use me. I'm not going to be able to witness to anyone. I'm not going to be able to say

177

---

anything to anyone about my faith or God's grace or anything else. I'm just so wounded. I'm of no use. But if I ever got healed of these wounds, I'd be something else. I just got to heal.'

You know the losers limp? You don't see it much in pro ball. But you do see it some in college. There's a lot in high school. The guy gets the ball and he is taking off to the goal post and this other guy gets after him. He realizes that he is just simply faster than me. I'm not going to be able to catch him. So what does he do? Charlie horse got my leg. But if it hadn't been for that, I would have caught him. Losers Limp. It's an excuse.

Moses used it. We all do. Paul said I'm wounded. It's a continuous wound. God would not take it away but God said to me, "My grace is sufficient," in the face of that wound. And then there are those of us who were wounded who use our wounds as an excuse and there are others of us who will use it as procrastination. "Just wait. I'm waiting till I'm healed. I'm waiting for a better time when things get better in my life. Maybe it's financial wounds and when the financial wounds are cured, I'll start giving more to God's work. 'Just wait. Oh, I'm going to do it. I really am going to do it but I got to be healed first. When I am healed, I'll do the work.

In Luke, two persons come to Jesus and want to follow him. Jesus said, "Wonderful! Come." One said, "Well, wait. Let me go home and bury my father." It's not that his father's already dead. He is saying I need to go home and take care of my father <u>until</u> he dies and then I'll follow you." The other one says, "Let me stay. Let me go home and say goodbye." Jesus says to both of them, "No. You just keep on going. If you're not willing to throw it all in for me, then just go on back to business. Go to do whatever you need to do.(Luke 9:57-62)

You know, I'm going to do a lot more for the Lord when I retire. Just wait. I'll have more time on my hands. Let me take a few more Spiritual Bible courses where I know a little more. Just wait.

Paul, in the face of his thorn, is a healer. It is in the presence of our woundedness, we are at our best.

Conclusion

A Jewish psychotherapist by the name of Yalom has been a mentor of mine for years through his writings. I've never met him personally. He's in his mid-70s today. One of his constant struggles was the fact he was a Willa. He had never been wounded. Wonderful parents, marvelous education, wonderful children, great-grandchildren, lucrative practice. He continually wrestled with how can these wounded people whom I deal with everyday relate to me when I'm not wounded. I don't know how many times in his books that I've read that he comes to this struggle and I'm saying to myself, "Your struggle Yalom is your wound. It is your struggle to identify, to understand, to be empathic with your clients." It is in our woundedness that we become wounded healers if we choose to. Wounds will make us better or bitter and you know both kind. You know those people who've been to "Hell and back" and out of their trauma and tragedy and thorns in life, they are just fabulous people who stand ready and willing for God's door of opportunity to be opened at any point in time. And then you know, and I know, those folks who've been wounded, traumatized, and they are bitter as quinine. They'll probably die like that.

It's our choice. Are we going to take our woundedness to the great wounded healer Jesus the Christ and say if you cannot remove it, if you will not remove it, may your grace be sufficient. In the midst of your gracefulness, use me to touch the lives of others. That's your choice. That is our hope. But out of our woundedness, out of our thorns, even with a skolops still in our life, we will be used by the Lord in ways that we could not otherwise be used. May it be true.

Let us pray.

O Lord, thank you for not answering Paul's prayer. Thank you for not taking the thorn out of his life. Thank you for, through the Spirit, bringing him to the realization that in the midst of his woundedness Your Grace was sufficient. Your grace is sufficient for us today if we in our woundedness will present ourselves to you as instruments to be used in your hands to the touch and healing of others. May we be available. In Jesus' name. Amen.

May God bless you and keep you healing.

WHAT HAPPENS TO US IS NOT THAT IMPORTANT.

**IT IS WHAT HAPPENS TO WHAT HAPPENS
TO US THAT IS IMPORTANT.**

Healing does not come from running away from our wounds, suffering and death.

Healing does not come from ignoring our wounds, suffering and death.

Healing does not even come from eliminating our wounds, suffering and death.

Healing comes in the very presence of our wounds, suffering and death.

~Gene Rollins

❧ ❀ ❧

CHAPTER 17

JESUS: OUR WOUNDED HEALER

Text: 1 Peter 2:21-25

CIT: *(Central Idea of the text)*
Jesus was wounded unjustly and through his unjust wounds we are justified.

Thesis: Jesus is our Wounded Healer whose mercy heals our wounds and whose grace empowers us to heal others.

Purpose:
- Major Objective: Evangelistic
- Specific Objective: Through the power of the Holy Spirit, I hope to lead each of us in receiving Jesus' healing.

Introduction

Outline:
   I.   Jesus' Wounds Were Unjust - v.22
   II.   Jesus' Wounds Did Not Cause Retaliation - v.23
   III.   Jesus' Wounds Were For Our Healing - v.24
   IV.   Jesus' Woundedness Serves As Our Example - vs.21-25

Conclusion:

"We, like Jesus,
have a choice –
whether or not
out of our woundedness
we are going to become
bitter,
resentful,
rageful,
and revengeful,
imparting our wounds
on other people."

The Word of the Lord

1 Peter 2:21-25

21 To this you were called, because Christ suffered for you, leaving you an example, that you should follow in his steps.

22 "He committed no sin, and no deceit was found in his mouth."

23 When they hurled their insults at him, he did not retaliate; when he suffered, he made no threats. Instead, he entrusted himself to him who judges justly. 24 He himself bore our sins in his body on the tree, so that we might die to sin and live for righteousness; by his wounds you have been healed. 25 For you were like sheep going astray, but now you have returned to the Shepherd and Overseer of your souls.

Introduction

I have said throughout the summer that all of us are wounded in some way to some degree. It is the wounds that we share that can be very productive to our own lives and to the lives of others if we realize that wounded connection.

Many of my congregation send me emails from time to time. Some are helpful; some are not. Some I can use in the pulpit and some I cannot. This story came to me a few weeks ago from one of our members. I'll share it filtering it through my own filters.

"Once upon a time a mouse lived in this farmer's house and the mouse observed through a crack in the wall that Mr. and Mrs. Farmer had brought a package home. He wondered what kind of food was in this package. So he watched through the crack as Mr. and Mrs. Farmer opened up this package. Lo and behold, to his shock and dismay the package contained a mousetrap. He was terrified. He ran out of the house screaming, 'There's a mouse trap in the house. There's a mouse trap in the house.' The first one he got to on the farmyard was a chicken. He said to the chicken, 'There's a mouse trap in the house; there's a mouse trap in the house.' The chicken said, 'Well, I hear your excitement and your dismay, but it's in the house. It is no skin off my nose.' So, getting no understanding or sympathy, the mouse moved on in the farmyard to the pig. He said to Mr. Pig, 'There's a mouse trap in the house; a mouse trap in the house.' Mr. Pig said, 'I feel your pain and I'll tell you what. I'll be praying for you. There's not much else I can do, Mr. Mouse.' So, he goes on through the barnyard to Mrs. Cow and he says to Mrs. Cow, 'There's a mouse trap in the house; there's a mouse trap in the house.' Mrs. Cow said to him, 'I'm sorry about that but it is really of no consequence to me.' So, dropping his little head in desperation the little mouse goes back in the house, back into his little bed. In dismay. In depression.

"During the night, sure enough the sound of a mouse trap, cracking. Mrs. Farmer got up in the darkness of the night to go check the mousetrap. Sure enough, it had sprung. In its trap was the tail of a Western Diamondback Rattlesnake. Unbeknownst to her, she reached down and the large rattlesnake bit her on the arm. Totally upset and dismayed and disarrayed in their house Mr. Farmer takes his wife to the hospital and brings her back in a day. She's still running a very high fever. Everybody knows what you do for a fever. You fix chicken soup! So, the farmer takes a hatchet and goes out into the barnyard and lops off the head of the chicken and brings the chicken in the house and fixes chicken soup for Mrs. Farmer. Well, the fever does not break. She does not do well. All the children come home. The neighbors come in. To feed them, Mr. Farmer goes out and slaughters the pig. She continues to worsen and dies. Many people come in from all around. The farmer needs more food and he has the cow slaughtered. Mr. Mouse observes all of this in great dismay." The moral of that story is self evident: we are in this together, folks. What affects you, affects me. My wounds are important and must be important to you. Your wounds must be important to me because we are on this wounded planet together.

The effects of everything are like ripples on this lake. They come all the way to the shore of Eternity. All of us are wounded. Our Savior was wounded. God observed our woundedness to the degree that the compassion poured forth and God said, "I must do something about my Creation's woundedness." So, Jesus Christ the Savior came, lived among us and was wounded, insulted, mistreated. We are the same. Often mistreated, insulted, abused and wounded through disease, darkness, death and many others.

In His woundedness, the Scriptures tell us he did not retaliate.

In the language of this summer, Jesus did not become a wounded - What? - wounder. We, like Jesus, have a choice - whether or not out of our woundedness we are going to become bitter, resentful, rageful, and revengeful, imparting our wounds on the other people. I don't care what those wounds are. I don't care when you received them. Even as a child in a dysfunctional family, I don't care what those wounds are. You have a choice. We have a choice. Are these wounds going to define me? Am I going to live out of these wounds the rest of my day and let them color every decision I make, every thought I have, every action I take? Am I going to do that? You have a choice. The choice is yours.

In this beautiful text the Scripture says through Peter, Jesus IS our example. Hupogrammos is the Greek word for the word we translated as example. But, example leaves a lot to be desired in the true meaning of that Greek word hupogrammos. It could better be translated 'pattern.'

I remember my mama, when she would prepare to sew a garment, she always had a pattern. It was a thin paper called onion skin paper. She would spread out that onion skin pattern. I remember her saying to me, "if my cloth is precisely the size and shape of this pattern, I will sew it well and it will be a good garment." The pattern made all the difference in the world. Following that pattern, every curve, every angle, meant the world in the outcome of that piece of cloth.

The scripture is telling us hupogrammos, Jesus IS our pattern. He IS our example. If you want to use the more current word, I think it also captures the meaning that Jesus is our paradigm. In a paradigm used today is that pattern of thinking that we carry with us. Jesus would have us to carry that pattern, that Paradigm of thinking with us as he suffered and did not retaliate and become a wounded wounder. He would have us in our wounds and in our suffering, not to retaliate and become wounded wounders.

Another term that you could put there, Jesus is our standard. So in life, the scripture tells us that Jesus is our paradigm, pattern, example, standard. This magnificent text tells us something else very important, too. In death, Jesus is our substitute. He bore our sins on the tree and by his wounds we are healed.

That beautiful 147th Psalm, verse 3 says, "He heals the brokenhearted and binds up their wounds." Can we really believe that? Can we really believe that God in Christ desires to heal us, bind up our wounds? If we believe that and we truly take them to him, then the scripture will become a fulfillment of its own promise.

In Jeremiah 8:22 the prophet is amazed. This is what the prophet says in that text. Three questions. "Is there no balm in Gilead?" Balm meaning healing salve. "Is there no physician there? Why then is there no healing for the wound of my people?" Wow! The healer is there. We must believe that Jesus is our substitutional atonement. That in his death, our death was taken. The great and ultimate wound that life will inflict upon us, Jesus has already taken. But it's not just that end wound. It is the wounds that we experience today, yesterday, and tomorrow.

In the little book Next Door Savior there's a chapter entitled The Trash Man. Max Lucado, in his little book, talks about this town that was smut-covered, dark, desolate. Every person in this town humped over, carrying this big Hefty bag, dragging it around filled with wounds. Here's a woman dragging a bag filled with guilt. Here is the young man dragging a bag filled with dysfunctional family early beginnings, and on and on the bags go filled with burdens and wounds. The people are raw from handling them; in despair from dragging them. The whole town is filled with persons just like that.

Lo and behold, one day a young 30 year old man shows up who has no bag. He's carrying no Hefty trash bag filled with guilt and shame and grief, gut-wrenching wounds. He invites the people as he circulates through the town to come out on Friday to the landfill and bring their bags of wounds and garbage with them. They don't know what's going on. They don't understand it. But the message spreads throughout this darkened little town. On Friday the people start taking their bags of guilt, grief, shame, and gore to the trash bin. There's the young man on his knees. The first woman comes to him. He has to implore her to dump her bag of guilt, grief, shame, and gut-wrenching wounds upon his head. As she does, he groans. Then another comes and another and another until the trash has covered this young strong 30 year old. All they can hear under that huge pile of trash is groans, moans, tears and agony. Then the sounds stop. For three days the people at the bottom of the hill wonder if they did the right thing by dumping all their grief and sorrow, shame and gore onto this young stranger. Then early the morning of the third day, one of the women looks upon the hill and cries out, "he's standing." They look up. In the middle of the trash and he stands tall, strong, vibrant once again the young man. [37] That is our story book. That is our story. Jesus is our trash man who says to us, "I will heal your wounds."

This verse 24 is absolutely magnificent. I would love to just camp out here. It says you have been healed. I know this means nothing to you but In the Greek it is a first aorist passive participle, meaning this: your wounds have been healed and are in the process of being healed. In other words, it is not just the wound yesterday. It is the wound that will be inflicted upon me today and tomorrow that has already been healed. In God's understanding, the healing has already taken place and will continue to take place.

When we realize that all the crap that we've been dealt and we deal with, God wants to take upon the cross and heal it. He wants us to feel that healing and to know that in our healing He is our example. We do not have to carry that. We do not have to perpetuate it. We can become wounded Healers. We can then, as Jesus did, wounded as He was, reach out to heal other people. Wounded as we are... not have been...ARE, wounded as we are, we can reach out and help the wounds of other people.

Conclusion

It is my deep heartfelt prayer that because of this summer and because of the healing within you, you will determine within your heart, mind and spirit to be Healers, no longer perpetuating your anger, your grief, your shame, onto anyone else but realizing, I have been forgiven. I am being healed and I want my forgiveness in my healing to be shared with everyone around me. What a world the world right around you could be.

Jesus is our standard in life. He is our substitute in death. He is our savior, the overseer of our souls in heaven. We are, you are, in his hands.

Let us pray.

---

[37] Lucado, Max. *Next Door Savior: Near Enough to Touch, Strong Enough to Trust.* 2006

Oh Lord, thank you that you loved us enough, came to become one of us and in becoming one of us, was horribly, horribly wounded unto death. A death that is not yours. A death that was for us. And in your death, "by your stripes" we are and will be continuously healed. May we share, live out the glory of that healing. In Jesus' name. Amen.

WHAT HAPPENS TO US IS NOT THAT IMPORTANT.

IT IS WHAT HAPPENS TO WHAT HAPPENS TO US THAT IS IMPORTANT.

Stephen William Hawking (Jan. 8, 1942 – Mar. 14, 2018). His university education began in 1959 at the age of 17 at University College, Oxford England. In 1962 he received his degree in Physics and began his graduate work at Trinity Hall, Cambridge. In 1963 life tumbled in upon Stephen Hawking with the diagnosis of "Lou Gehrigs Disease." He was given two years to live. When life tumbles in, what then? What then is the rest of the story. Wounded with this horrible disease for 55 years, yet, in the field of science his name is a household word. Working as a theoretical physicist, cosmologist and author he has been a major person in the healing of "Mother Earth." His work in the education of climate change was noted when he received the "Presidential Medal of Freedom" in 2009. In 2002 he was ranked number 25 in the "BBCs" poll of the 100 Greatest Britons. His ashes are placed in Westminster Abbey's Nave between Sir Isaac Newton and Charles Darwin.

CONCLUSION

WHEN LIFE TUMBLES IN, WHAT THEN?

Text: Job 1:13-22

CIT: *(Central Idea of the text)*
Job's life tumbled in upon him loosing his family and all of his wealth.

Thesis: Life is going to tumble in upon you, and what will you do then?

Purpose:

- Major Objective: Supportive
- Specific Objective: Through the power of the Holy Spirit I hope to lead each of us in receiving our trials and tribulations as opportunities for healing.

Introduction

Outline:
    I.   We May Become Bitter Blaming God And Others
    II.   We May Try Living As If They Are Not Real
   III. We May Simply Attempt To Endure
  IV. We May Discover The Power And Presence Of A Healing God

Conclusion

"God does not
cause
our suffering.

God does not
cancel
our suffering.

God is
companioning
with us in our
suffering."

The Word of the Lord

Job 1:13-22

One day when Job's sons and daughters were feasting and drinking wine at the oldest brother's house, 14 a messenger came to Job and said, "The oxen were plowing and the donkeys were grazing nearby 15 and the Sabeans attacked and carried them off. They put the servants to the sword, and I am the only one who has escaped to tell you!"

16 While he was still speaking, another messenger came and said, "The fire of God fell from the sky and burned up the sheep and the servants, and I am the only one who has escaped to tell you!"

17 While he was still speaking, another messenger came and said, "The Chaldeans formed three raiding parties and swept down on your camels and carried them off. They put the servants to the sword, and I am the only one who has escaped to tell you!"

18 While he was still speaking, yet another messenger came and said, "Your sons and daughters were feasting and drinking wine at the oldest brother's house, 19 when suddenly a mighty wind swept in from the desert and struck the four corners of the house. It collapsed on them and they were dead, and I am the only one who has escaped to tell you!"

20 At this, Job got up and tore his robe and shaved his head. Then he fell to the ground in worship 21 and said:

"Naked I came from my mother's womb, and naked, I will depart. The LORD gave and the LORD has taken away; may the name of the LORD be praised."

22 In all this, Job did not sin by charging God with wrongdoing.

May God bless and illuminate God's Word.

When Life Tumbles In, What Then? Notice the title does not say 'if' life tumbles in. You can be assured life 'will' tumble in on you at some point in time.

Introduction

As I write this last chapter it is April 28, 2020. Life has truly tumbled in upon us. The "Corona Virus Disease" has tumbled in upon us. As of today, worldwide there are 2.99 million cases with 208,000 deaths. In the US there are 989,000 cases with 55,551 deaths. In my state of South Carolina there are 5,253 cases with 166 deaths. In my small county there are 205 cases and 9 deaths, one of which was a friend of mine.

I have not been to my downtown offices in four weeks. Along with most everyone else I am hunkered down at home. 2.6 million people are out of work and may have lost their jobs. Life has tumbled in!

How many times have I said when death hits or some other form of tribulation comes: "As the people of God we gather together and tell the story of who we are and whose we are." But today we cannot do that! We cannot gather in our places of worship. We cannot go to our places of security, sanctity and shalom. Life has tumbled in upon us.

Job was a good man living a good life. All of a sudden, his life begins to fall in upon him. Two outside forces, the Sabeans and the Chaldeans, come in as raiding parties and take away his flocks and kill all of his servants. Lightning strikes, 'an Act of God' we call that, and his sheep and servants were killed. Another 'Act of God,' a tornado, comes to the house where his ten children are having a party together and they are all killed and their families and servants. Job is left without wealth, without property and without family. One whose life was good. One whose life was healthy, wealthy and wise, all of a sudden finds himself without anything. Devastated. Everything in his life has been taken away.

When life tumbles in as it did plummet in on Job, what do we then do? Life tumbles in, in many ways. Like when that spouse says, "I need to talk with you. Things are not well. I'm no longer happy. We need to separate." Life tumbles in.

When you go to the doctor for a normal, routine checkup and the doctor says, "We need to do more testing." Finally, the doctor says, "You have been diagnosed with a malignancy and it does not look good." Life has tumbled in.

When you get that call in the middle of the night that you never want to receive, the child says, "I've been locked up for the possession and distribution of drugs."

Or that call from another part of the state or nation says, "You need to make arrangements to come. Your family is in trouble."

In many sundry ways, life just simply tumbles in upon us. It may be the loss of our wealth. It may be the loss of our vocation. It may be the loss of our spouse. But whatever losses come, they always come in one form or another, life tumbles upon all of us.

Voltaire's doubts begin to tumble in upon him, that great thinker of yesterday, and he said, "I wish to God I had never been born."

They tumbled in on that brilliant Englishman, Oscar Wilde, and he looked out on the streets of London and said, "There is enough violence, crime, hurt and hatred on the streets of London to disprove God in any day." Surely, if Wilde could say it of his day in England, when we look on our streets of today, how much more so could we make that statement.

What happens when life tumbles in upon us?

Moses goes upon a mountain, fellowshipping with God, receiving the Ten Commandments, only to come back down below and he finds his people in a drunken, sexual, idolatry orgy around a golden calf. Moses' life tumbles in upon him. He saw his leadership crumble.

David's kingdom is going well until the prophet Nathan sticks his long finger in his face, "David, you are the man." And, David's life crumbles around him as he knows the world knows his innermost secrets.

Jesus cries out in the Garden of Gethsemane, after a betrayal kiss to the cheek, when the soldiers come to arrest him.

Life falls in on all of us in one way or another. And, then comes the more important question: when life tumbles in, what then? Some of us just blame God. Some of us cry out deep from within, "Why me oh God? Why is this happening?" In fact, Job does that. Job understands that life tumbling in on him as God's act. Job says, "The Lord gave and now the Lord has taken away."

There are those of us that live with that kind of philosophy that no matter what happens, God caused it.

I was deeply disturbed several years ago when I heard a portion of the funeral for the Smith children in Union, S.C. One of the ministers in his prayer at that funeral said, "We wanted the boys to be with us, but God wanted them to begin an eternity with Him." In other words, this horrible tragedy is God's Will. This horrible tragedy has been caused by God. Somehow God wanted these children more than we

195

wanted these children. What we do with those kinds of understandings is that we do not follow through. Because what we do with those kinds of understandings is say that God is a murderer! And the position we place people in is that out of one side of our mouths we're saying if it's a horrible time of tragedy or when life has fallen in on you, turn to God. And, then out of the other side of our mouths we say God has caused this tragedy in your life.

There are those of us who blame God. There are those of us who blame others - God and everyone else around us. There's always someone who has caused this.

My little grandsons were here this weekend. There was a debate as to whether Papa was going to let them go hunting with him or not because each one of them made a D on their report card. They did make some A's in other stuff but they each had this one D that stood out like a red light. So, as I was talking yesterday with the eldest grandson who is 13 years old, I asked him about this D. He said the teacher didn't like him. I said, "That's all you got to say about this D is that the teacher doesn't like you?"

It is always someone else's fault, someone else's to blame. Usually, that someone else begins with God. When life begins to tumble in on us there are those of us who simply blame God.

Then, there are those of us who try to live as if it is not really happening. We call that denial. When life tumbles in, we won't deal with it. We'll just go on living like it hasn't tumbled in on us. I see that often at the hospital. Someone will receive a horrible diagnosis and a terrible prognosis and the nurse will say as she calls the chaplain for that department, "It might be well to go by to see Ms. Smith." The chaplain goes by to see her and asks, "Ms. Smith, how are you today?" And, she says, "Oh, I'm doing fine."

"Well, how is your health?" "I'm going to be ok," she says.

It's a coping mechanism. But when life tumbles in on us, we often use it. Somehow denying the very fact that we've been told that our life is hanging by a thread, we just smile and say, "Well, I don't know that I believe that." Denial serves a purpose to a point. But there comes a point when life has tumbled in around us, we must simply admit that life has caved in.

Then there are those of us who simply endure it. It is kind of like fate. Whatever is going to be is going to be. 'Que Sera, Sera.' I love that statement a British man said years ago, "Life ain't what you want it to be but it is all you're going to get. So, just put a geranium in your hat and be happy." It's like that good Presbyterian who fell down a long flight of stairs and as he landed on the bottom, he got up and dusted himself off and said, "Praise God that's over!" It just had to happen. That's fate. There are those of us, when life tumbles in, who just simply bites the lower lip and endures. This is something that just had to happen, and it has happened, and I am just going to live through it.

But I believe there is another option. When life begins to cave in on us, I believe there's another option. That is to accept the reality of what's taking place, not live in denial. To accept the fact that God does not cause everything that happens. Sometimes our own dumb choices put us in those positions. Sometimes the choices of others put us in that position. Sometimes just by simple chance we happen to be at the wrong place at the wrong time or whatever, it just happens. But to blame no one, just simply experience the mystery of what has happened. To believe in the midst of this tumbling in of life, that somehow through the power of prayer and through the presence of God, not only are we going to endure this, but that we are going to experience this in such a way that our lives are going to be enriched and matured through this horrible experience. We can become a wounded healer.

Job experiences that in the end. It takes him a long time to get there but in chapter 42 Job says, "Surely, I spoke of things I did not understand, things too wonderful for me to know. My ears had heard of you but now my eyes have seen you." In other words, Job came to the point where he did not understand why he was suffering as he was but he no longer blamed God for it. He began to see God in ways he had not seen God before. I believe that therein is our potential in the midst of those quick turns of events, when life begins to tumble in on us, is to believe that God, too, is in the midst of it. Not causing and not even canceling, God is companioning with us in the midst of this horrible experience. We will through God's presence and through the power of prayer begin to develop a newer and deeper relationship with God.

I remember so well the words of Paul. He had that thorn in the flesh, whatever it was. He said, I prayed and I prayed and I asked God to remove this. God wouldn't. But Paul said that through the midst of this experience I realized that God's power was made perfect in the presence of my weakness. In other words, what Paul was saying, "I came to realize that I couldn't trust my own strength, my own ability. I had to lean on God. I began to trust God in new and different ways."

In James 1:2-3, the text says, "count it as a joy when life tumbles in on us." Boy, that's hard to do. James says count it as a joy for this reason. As these trials and tribulations come down upon you, and as you trust in the power and presence of God through prayer, that your life will deepen and perseverance will be developed.

I love that Hebrew word that is translated as perseverance. It is two Greek words made into one. "Huppo," which means under; "mino" means sustains. What the word is saying is that when life tumbles in upon us and we continue to believe and we continue to embrace our faith and we continue to call upon the presence of God, then we develop a character that will stand under the pressures of life. We will develop a maturity of life that will not give way. We develop a faith that will stand.

I wear a different stole today. It's one I've had for four years now. It was given to me by the family of a dear friend of mine, Charlie Newman. He was a Methodist minister, a colleague. Life fell in on Charlie. Charlie couldn't take it. He went to a motel room and consumed enough pills to kill two persons and then shot himself, the ultimate anger response to a tumbling in of life. That's always our choice.

What happens to us is not that important. It is what happens to what happens to us. What happens to us happens to everybody. Nothing is more universal than suffering. Nothing is more common than the tumbling in of life. So that's not important. It's not important what happens. <u>What is life-changingly important is what happens to what happens to us.</u> It is taking this falling in of life saying, "God, I don't understand this. I don't understand why this has happened. I don't understand how this has happened. I don't understand how I have gotten myself into this situation I am in but I believe you are in this situation with me. I don't know what is going to come out of it. But I am trusting you to be in it with me and to walk hand in hand and heart in heart with me. I'm trusting you to bring something new and different out of it. One of the things that will become new and different is a character that is able to stand under the pressures of life. Perseverance. I don't know any other way perseverance is developed other than through hardship. I don't know any other way that endurance is developed other than through difficulties. It is in those hardships and difficult times as we continue to believe that somehow God is in this and that God is somehow going to use this and somehow we are being perfected in the midst of this.

Conclusion

That beautiful eighth chapter of Romans where the scripture says, nothing happens to us uselessly. But everything that happens to us, God can use for our nurturing, for our maturing and for our good. Please don't mistranslate that verse. That verse did not say that God causes everything. It didn't say that at all. We so often misinterpret that verse. The verse says, whatever happens to us God can use for our good and God's glory. But if we get stuck on what happens to us, if we do not turn our attention upon what can happen to what happens to us, there's where we become stuck. There's where we stay. There's where we become so disappointed, depressed that we do the ultimate of what Charlie Newman did.

When we can cry deep within ourselves: "What is happening is horrible. What is happening is devastating, but what's more important is what I let happen to what's happened."

Job blamed God. God gives and God takes away. But in the midst of that Job yet says, God gave and God took away. Blessed be the name of the Lord. One thing we will find Job not loosing in the midst of all his losses is his faith. He doubts it. He struggles with it. He confronts God with it. But he never looses his faith. And in the end comes to say to God, I now know you in ways that I never knew you before. I believe he is also saying, I now understand myself in ways that I never understood before.

When life tumbles in and we trust the presence of God and believe in the power of prayer we can stand. Then, what happens to what happens to us becomes extremely important.

Let us pray:

Oh, Lord we sure doubt the abundant life is not ours when good things are not happening and good things are going awry. Our dreams are crumbling, our plans are falling apart. Oh, God, that's when our faith, tested - yes, that's when our faith becomes mature. That's when our lives deepen. That's when our character is built. That's when our perseverance develops. Oh, God, it is hard to do what you say, to count these days as joy days. So forgive us for whining, for complaining, blaming, doubting. In the midst of, help us to maintain our faith. In maintaining we will persevere. In Jesus' name. Amen.

May God bless you and keep you. Keep you persevering in the midst of your trials. May God also heal your wounds helping you to become a wounded healer.

A SIMPLE EXAMPLE OF BEING
A WOUNDED HEALER

Dear Mrs.

I am putting some of the things we talked about today in print so that you can refer back to them and give them more thought.

First about the mantra: It is the oldest mantra we have in written form. Here it is again:

"That is not mine." Everyone outside of yourself is a "that." Your husband is a "that." You cannot fix him, change him or alter him in any way. You have tried that for years and all it has gotten is conflict. You cannot change him with your love, with your anger, with your nagging or with your sweetness. He is a "that!" "That" is not yours.

Your daughter is a "that." She became a "that" when she became an adult. The window for you to change her closed when she became about age 12. Now, you relate to her first and foremost as an adult to another adult. Now, she is a "that." You spend all of your energy on trying to change these two "that's" within your life and you have no energy left to work on yourself. And yourself is the only place where your energy has any affect. Therefore, stop focusing on them and focus upon yourself. I know, you want them to change and I assure you they will but only in response to the changes that you make within yourself.

As I shared with you, I tried my best to change my first wife of 25 years. I knew what was best for us if she would only change and become who I wanted her to become. She would not, so when the last child graduated from high school I moved out and divorced her. Three years later I married a beautiful and wonderful woman. But she had just a few things I wanted her to change, and so some struggles began. Thank God in my research I found this mantra: "that is not mine." My wife became a "that." I spend my energy working on me and not her. Yes, I backslide from time to time but that is what a mantra is. We keep it on the front of our mind to repeat many times during the day.

Second, when you blame your husband and your daughter you only get defensiveness from them. It is true for all of us, when we blame we defend. When they blame you what do you do? Defend yourself. So stop blaming them and when they blame you try not to become defensive. When this does happen, one or all three of you withdraw. You must stop the cycle and stay connected. Keep talking. Talk it through without blame or defensiveness.

The third thing we talked about was working on defining who you are. I gave you the example of my self-definition related to blame. My father died in front of the family when he was only 42 years of age and I was only 4. My family believed that nothing happens without God's will being done. For me that meant that God killed my daddy with this heart attack. I was one angry child and youth. If one can be angry at the ultimate authority it is nothing to be angry and defiant at lesser authorities; therefore, I stayed in trouble with my parent, teachers and the law. There came a time when I began to self-define, disbelieving what my family believed and blamed heart disease rather than God for my father's death. Disease carries us to God and God welcomes us. Begin to look at yourself in the context of your family of origin and define who you are, not who they are or maybe who they wanted you to be.

Please think over what we said and read over what I recapped for us and we will continue our work together next week.

Shalom,

Dr. Rollins

Selected Bibliography
for Future Reading

I would recommend all of the books referred to in my footnotes.

1. Anderson, Greg. The 22 Non-Negotiable Laws of Wellness. New York: Harper Collins Publishers, 1995.
2. Barasch, Marc Ian. The Healing Path. New York: Penguin Books, 1994.
3. Barker, Robert L. The Green-Eyed Marriage. New York: The Free Press. 1987
4. Bly, Robert, Hillman, James, Meade, Michael, Eds. The Rag and Bone Shop of the Heart. New York: Harper Collins Publishers. 1992.
5. Chard, Philip Sutton. The Healing Earth. Minocqua, WI: North Word Press, 1994.
6. Cousins, Norman. The Healing Heart. New York: WW Norton and Company, 1983.
7. Judy, Dwight H. Healing the Male Soul. New York: Crossroad. 1992.
8. Ornstein, Robert and Swencionis, Charles, Ed. Healing Brain. New York: The Guilford Press, 1990.
9. Wibber, Ken. Grace and Grit. Boston: Shambhala, 1991

Printed in the United States
By Bookmasters